The
World
On
Time®

The 11 Management Principles
That Made FedEx
an Overnight Sensation

James C. Wetherbe

KNOWLEDGE EXCHANGE  SANTA MONICA, CALIFORNIA

To my family:

Jessie, Jamie and Smoky

Contents

Memphis
'Round Midnight

Memphis, around midnight. The men and women boarding the bus late are a new breed of tourist—the industrial sightseer. Twice a month, fresh contingents of travelers willingly pay $250 each for the privilege of spending several hours in the operational heart of Federal Express Corporation. They come to learn firsthand how in 23 years the company has grown from a trailblazing start-up—it literally invented the overnight package-delivery business—to a $10-billion industry leader of mythic proportions.

Today, in 1996, FedEx employs more than 120,000 people. It flies 500-plus planes, drives almost 36,000 vehicles, and hauls in excess of two million pounds of air freight every 24 hours.

No wonder businesspeople from every continent sign up for this world-renowned, late-night floor show. Tonight's busload includes two visitors from Arizona (executives of a large utility); a dozen or so Brazilians (including the head of a refrigerator compressor manufacturer); a half-dozen Mexicans (senior managers from a transportation conglomerate, also in the overnight package-delivery business); and 12 Argentines (businesspeople gathered together by a tour operator specializing in industrial sites).

The visitors are full of anticipation. Several lean forward and cup their hands against the windows for a better view. The tourists are surprised that traffic is clogging up the four-lane approach to the FedEx facility.

"Gridlock at 11:00 p.m.?" one asks.

As their bus inches closer to its destination, the visitors can distinguish the looming outlines of a vast, flood-lit complex. This is what they've come to see—the SuperHub, operational heart of the FedEx empire. Every night, packages that FedEx couriers picked up only a few hours earlier, arrive at the SuperHub where sorters direct them to the FedEx aircraft, trucks, and vans that will deliver them to their appointed destinations.

Over the next two hours, the SuperHub's dozens of miles of concrete taxiways will accommodate the unloading and reloading of 135 airplanes—ranging from mammoth McDonnell Douglas MD-11s to small, short-hop Cessna 208s. The hangar-like SuperHub houses acres of crisscrossing conveyor belts, metal slides, and package-sorting tables. Thousands of part-time sorters, scanners, tractor drivers, and ground crew are streaming into the four-story building. The midnight traffic snarl suddenly makes sense. The bus finally turns into a parking lot.

IN THE DIN OF THE NIGHT

The travelers crowd into the enormous reception area of the already bustling package-screening facility and accept mugs of steaming coffee. They take a moment to inspect an imposing FedEx icon, one of the company's original Falcon jets. Then they head for the escalator that carries them to an observation point.

The structure is like a giant beehive. Several stories below, navy-and-orange-clad men and women steer tractors and forklifts among the package-sorting stations. Others launch clanging metal containers onto conveyor belts that snake through the tumult. Obviously they all know exactly what they're doing, but to the visitors it looks chaotic. Outside, in the sky, the first of the incoming jets banks for landing.

At the facility's center, behind the closed doors of a room known as "the hot seat," managers keep a steady watch on the army of workers. They have only two and a half hours to unload more than one million packages from the planes, then sort and direct them for shipment. Television monitors, hundreds of them, are everywhere. In the corner of the screens, "Sno-Con One" flashes an ominous warning. The first snowfall of the season is forecast. The television screens are high-tech digital hourglasses counting down the seconds since the arrival of the first plane. They're telling everyone what must be done by when.

Annie Austin leads the visitors through the noisy scene. A FedEx document scanner and volunteer guide, she warns them to stand clear of the forklifts, cargo tugs, and tractors wheeling in and out of the building. This is her turf. Like so many other FedEx employees, Austin started at FedEx as a part-time college student working for extra spending money. After graduation she signed on full-time.

So far the weather is holding. The planes are landing every 45 seconds. The moment a pilot kills the engine, the race to unload the plane begins. It rarely takes more than 30 minutes. Raising her voice above the din, Austin explains that the SuperHub replaced the original facility in 1984, and in 1987 a second major hub opened a few hundred miles away in Indianapolis. FedEx also has scattered regional hubs along both coasts, in Newark, Miami, Fort Worth,

Oakland, Los Angeles, Anchorage, and abroad in the Philippines, Dubai, and Paris.

Every night, Austin says, the SuperHub's 171 miles of conveyor belts send packages down slides, through diverters, under measurement lasers, and past sorters. The group's attention zeros in on a sorter who grabs a package off one belt, reads its bar code with an infrared scanner, and places it onto another belt. The package progresses past other sorters, who direct it to waiting tractors and containers. Sorters must know by heart the entire list of three-letter codes FedEx uses to expedite the process. "There is no other way," Austin explains, "to meet the sort target of 32 pieces per minute." As Austin speaks, the visitors from FedEx's Mexican competitor take notes.

"Please stay right behind me," Austin shouts. The visitors climb to a deck that overlooks the runways and docking stations. Here it is relatively quiet. Empty aircraft wait for their payloads and the return to home bases. Glancing at a nearby monitor, one of the visitors notes that almost all the clock digits are down to zero. "Was tonight's sort a success?" she asks.

"It looks as if everyone is finishing on time," Austin says. "We'll get all the details tomorrow morning when our in-house TV station, FXTV, broadcasts 'FedEx Overnight.'"

As they wait for the bus that will return them to their hotel, some of the tourists—looking weary from their three-hour adventure—linger to chat with Austin. A few flakes of snow are just starting to fall. "What will happen," an Argentine woman asks, "if this turns into a blizzard?"

"If there's an emergency," Austin says, "we've got generators here that will keep the equipment running so that we can continue to sort packages efficiently."

I make my living helping people break the barriers between the technical and human sides of their organizations. I've worked with some of the largest and best-known corporations in the world— among them, AT&T, NCR, Apple, Hewlett-Packard, IBM, 3M, Georgia-Pacific, Pillsbury, General Mills, and Motorola. And I've written some 15 books that describe what I've found out.

Since 1993, as the first Federal Express Professor of Excellence at the University of Memphis, I've studied the FedEx way of doing business. Part of my job, through the Center for Cycle Time Research, is entirely practical. It consists of providing diagnostic services and prescriptive solutions to the logistical challenges— ranging from inventory management to delivery schedules—that confront FedEx customers.

I have also had the opportunity to work with Fred Smith, the company's founder, chairman, and CEO, and other senior executives. I've analyzed FedEx's history, its philosophy, and its systems, as well as its ability to transform strategic decisions into profitable operations. I've studied the company from top to bottom. I can confirm that Fred Smith has created one of the extraordinary companies in the history of American business.

The FedEx story demonstrates how one determined person, started with a bright idea—an idea, incidentally, that academicians and businesspeople scoffed at—and created a billion-dollar global giant. Its innovative management strategies have revolutionized the way modern companies manage time and information, plan complex logistics, and serve customers to generate customer loyalty.

By 1990, the general public already equated FedEx with dependability, punctuality, and overall quality service. At the same time, it inspired competition in a cutthroat marketplace. The Postal Service grew especially apprehensive. In 1994, Postmaster General

Marvin Runyon felt compelled to write a letter to *Business Week* asserting that "the expedited-mail marketplace was started by the U.S. Postal Service in 1970 and not by Federal Express Corp. Indeed, we helped Federal Express in the 1970s when it carried U.S. Mail."

Was ever a protest a sweeter compliment?

In this book I aim to show why Marvin Runyon and others have had so much to say about FedEx. I examine both FedEx's successes and its few failures—from which it learned so much—I have extracted abiding management principles that help guide FedEx. These principles, I believe, can help managers of virtually any company, in any industry, at any point in its history.

I am deeply indebted to the many fine people at Federal Express for their help and support. This book is a tribute to their accomplishments.

Over the last three years or so, I have conducted extensive research and hundreds of interviews. I have discerned why—or, better yet, how—FedEx has maintained its profitable commitment to excellence. I believe that if your company is similarly committed, you would do well to embrace the 11 principles that underlie the unparalleled success of Federal Express. Here they are:

- You can never, ever, do enough for your people.

- Everybody pitches in.

- Rewards are absolutely, positively everything.

- A winning culture has many cultures.

- An ounce of inspiration is worth a pound of control.

- The first rule is change the rules.

- Problems have silver linings, too.

- Software equals savings, service, *and* sales.

- He who hesitates is lost (but, remember, look before you leap).

- Letting go is hard to do.

- The image is the reality (if you work at it).

Let me first offer a brief introduction to each of them.

You can never, ever, do enough for your people.

"The rights and value of a single human life," begins FedEx managers' training guide, "have become the central focus of social evolution in the industrialized world...FedEx, from its inception, has put its people first both because it is right to do so and because it is good business as well." And FedEx employees respond in kind. At the end of one pay period in the difficult early days of the company, employees received a memo along with their paychecks. The memo, from Fred Smith, stated that they were welcome to cash their checks, but, he suggested, it sure would be helpful if some of them waited just a few days. To this day, some of those checks remain uncashed. Their owners display them proudly, as a badge of honor, in frames on their FedEx office walls. Do your employees feel a similar sense of loyalty to your company?

Fred Smith knew from the start that if he put people first, quality, service, and profits would follow. He has created a flat management structure, minimizing the distance between leaders and frontline workers—a move that has empowered employees and expanded the breadth of their responsibilities.

Everybody pitches in.

FedEx has a basic principle: Everyone has specific responsibilities, but there are low fences between jobs. People will hop over fences to help others out, but nobody can blame another for his or her failures. Courier, sorter, pilot, or public-relations specialist—every FedEx employee should focus on the customer. Managers, including the senior vice presidents from Smith's inner circle, make personal sales calls, and during the holiday season they load and unload packages in the hubs. Sales representatives and operations personnel work hand in hand to achieve the common goal: the all-important FedEx guarantee. At the FedEx Orange Bowl, amidst the food and hoopla, company reps take advantage of FedEx's sponsorship to demonstrate new products and new technologies.

Rewards are absolutely, positively everything.

FedEx rewards success. For example, an employee who exceeds a customer's expectations may win on-the-spot recognition or rewards for a job well done. The company doesn't restrict reward giving to the annual review, nor is money the only kind of reward. The company continually invites employee and customer assessments. Is FedEx a good employer? Is the service what it should be? FXTV, the multimillion-dollar in-house station, broadcasts weekly and daily measurements of corporate results.

Everyone—from the chairman's office down—uses the data to plan and to evaluate track records. Such scoreboards allow FedEx to acknowledge performance with appropriate rewards.

A winning culture has many cultures.

FedEx's overall culture is famous for its attention to detail and its absolute dependability. FedEx customers know they will not be disappointed. They do not expect to be surprised. The company has gone to great lengths to assure that employees understand FedEx's goals, and all employees know, individually, what they have to do to reach those goals. In Memphis, people say, the FedEx employees bleed purple—the company's primary color.

FedEx stays ahead of the competition because it's not an infantry division, a mass of bodies moving in one direction. Rather, it's an aircraft carrier, an association of specialists running a complex mechanism. The company has many subcultures: On the floor of the SuperHub the culture is time; in the software development lab and logistics services the culture is innovation and ideas; in the field the culture is customer satisfaction. The conventional company has one culture only. I've seen high-tech companies whose sales culture dominated to the point that engineering was compromised. In such companies, they often lose the most talented engineers to the competition. Conversely, I've seen companies whose engineering culture was so strong it compromised understanding and responsiveness to customers. FedEx has one macroculture and grows many subcultures as well.

An ounce of inspiration is worth a pound of control.

FedEx managers are transformational leaders. Fred Smith knows that a manager earns employees' respect and allegiance only by leading with idealism and style. He marries that belief with his conviction that FedEx can sustain its high level of customer satisfaction only if its leaders understand employees' needs and expectations.

The company has designed its evaluation procedures and training programs to ensure that it develops leaders who know how to set the right examples. Its senior executives are the models for its up-and-coming managers.

The first rule is change the rules.

FedEx shook the package-delivery business when it discarded Postal Code–inspired zone-and-volume pricing systems in favor of fixed pricing. Confusion over charges all but disappeared. The change not only simplified processes at FedEx, but also allowed customers to project their shipping costs with accuracy. And when Smith convinced Congress to deregulate the air-express business, competitors shared the benefits, and industry revenues jumped tenfold.

Problems have silver linings, too.

FedEx, like all other innovators, regards every problem as a challenge to develop new technologies or services: Innovators transform problems into opportunities. FedEx welcomes its customers' problems as well.

A worldwide retailer of women's clothing and home furnishings had been trying to get a handle on its warehousing and distribution operations. Its CEO went to FedEx and asked its Logistics, Electronic Commerce and Catalog (LECC) department to use its unique tracking system to help track orders, inventory, and shipping schedules. Result: For the first time in its recent history, this retailer was able to provide 48-hour turnaround on orders. LECC proved that logistics expertise was a competitive advantage.

Software equals savings, service, *and* sales.

In the Information Age, companies that master technology will lead their industries and dominate their markets. In 1994, Fred Smith told a Harvard Business School interviewer that his company was the logistics arm of a whole new society, one "built around service industries and high-technology endeavors in electronics and optics and medical science." FedEx has proved—more conclusively than most other companies—that the information an organization creates and shapes has value far beyond its in-house uses. Starting with FedEx's software, which allows it to track shipments, the company has leveraged the strengths of its information management systems into a vastly profitable logistics-consulting business.

He who hesitates is lost (but, remember, look before you leap).

When Fred Smith decided to offer next-day afternoon delivery, his closest advisers fretted that it would cannibalize the existing priority and economy services. Smith argued that the new service would generate cash and eliminate FedEx's down periods between priority morning deliveries and the afternoon economy runs. He was confident that standard overnight service would make use of idle company assets without adding substantial costs. What's more, Smith maintained, if FedEx didn't grab the opportunity, the competition certainly would.

Smith's hunch paid off. Customers' enthusiasm for the new service was enormous, and two-day delivery has been growing while Priority Overnight has also continued to grow since its inception.

Letting go is hard to do.

Occasionally both gut instinct and spreadsheet models are wrong. ZapMail—FedEx's disappointing experiment in state-of-the-art, satellite-connected, faxed-document, to-the-door delivery—failed when low-cost fax machines flooded the business market. Within two years of its launch, FedEx shut ZapMail down, wrote off the losses, and reassigned thousands of ZapMail employees to other tasks. Nevertheless, because FedEx has from the start institution-alized risk-taking, other seemingly more implausible initiatives have succeeded—the first hub-and-spoke system, the proprietary fleet of aircraft, and TV ads about FedEx technology rather than package delivery, to name a few.

The image is the reality (if you work at it).

FedEx's guaranteed on-time service and complete satisfaction is unconditional. Customers equate FedEx with that promise. It is this image that the public identifies with FedEx—and it doesn't come easy. The image the company has so meticulously cultivated helps maintain, even extend, its market share. FedEx makes no excuses. Its highly successful advertising program reinforces that reputa-tion, and so does the pride employees take in their work.

In the following chapters, I describe and examine the impact of those 11 guiding management principles. Each of them, individually as well as collectively, has helped shape FedEx into the company that you know today: a company that defines the avant-garde of innovation and customer service.

CHAPTER 1

You Can Never, Ever, Do Enough for Your People

Does your organization have a no-layoff philosophy?

Does your company regularly survey employees to keep abreast of their needs? Is there a mechanism for acting on the concerns you identify?

Do your employees review the performance of their managers? Do their reviews have an impact on the managers' compensation?

Does your company make a sincere and ongoing effort to promote from within?

"You will never have good customer relations until you have good employee relations," was a key business philosophy of Walt Disney. Today, as the downsizings go on and on, and as the outsourcings become more and more inventive, expressions of devotion to employees get louder and louder. It's enough to turn a saint into a cynic.

Federal Express Corporation, in this respect, is a monument to sincerity and loyalty. Look behind every one of the company's commitments to its employees' interests—a no-layoffs philosophy; thoughtful and imaginative compensation schemes; continuing employee-training programs; a policy of promotion from within; a thorough dedication to procedural fairness in handling grievances; free, open, two-way communication systems; and, finally, keen attention to employee opinion—and you will find not a trace of hypocrisy, only strong conviction.

FedEx's famous slogan—People-Service-Profit—is a virtual circle. As the company's *Manager's Guide* puts it, "Each link [in the circle] upholds the others and is in turn upheld by them." And *people* is always understood to embrace both customers *and* employees. Thus, the employees provide unsurpassed service, which creates loyal customers, who supply excellent profits, which makes for a prosperous enterprise (and happy shareholders), which creates highly competent and motivated employees (who need not be laid off), who in turn provide unsurpassed service, and so on.

This circle logically begins with the employees. Unlike a product business (Walt's, say), a service business must have employees before it has customers or profits. How has FedEx created a company in which employees flourish? Let us count the ways.

THE JOB OF KEEPING JOBS— A NO-LAYOFFS POLICY

No company today can honestly make an unconditional commitment to a no-layoffs policy. Too much uncertainty exists—in markets, in competition, and in technological change—for any enterprise to guarantee jobs forever for all its people. IBM learned that lesson a few years ago; AT&T learned it too.

But what companies *can* do, and what FedEx does do, is make a commitment to reasonable employment security. Not absolute, just reasonable. The point is not so much the adjective, but the care and concern that go into the effort. At FedEx the effort is visible, earnest, and imaginative. That's why employees trust it. As Mary Alice Taylor, senior vice president for the United States and Canada, says: "Employees know that we will go to extremes to retain them." And because they know it, they flourish, and the company along with them.

But how, despite financial and competitive pressures, does FedEx do it?

Cross-Training. At FedEx, training—available to all capable and willing employees—prepares them for more than one job in the company. The result is a broadly trained workforce. The company benefits from this because top managers have flexibility in responding to changing workloads and shifting demands in skills. Employees benefit because the "other" job is insurance against technological obsolescence and temporary down ticks in the market for their present jobs. And both benefit in that employees are less fearful of automation or other causes of displacement, and the company can count on continuing high morale.

Redistributing Work. FedEx understands that work, like other goods, can be distributed and redistributed. For example, in the event of constricting markets (internal or external), FedEx will curtail overtime. People who have been working six days a week will cut back to five, with the unfilled time distributed to people who might otherwise not work at all.

Cultivating a Large Part-Time Workforce. "Rather than hire new full-time people for the peak hours and seasons, we expand part-time workers' hours," explains the senior vice president of personnel, James Perkins. "Then, after peak, when we reduce the hours, we won't have to lay anyone off." The work of a number of the part-timers might be called generic: Their skills are relatively common and can be supplied through temporary employment agencies. The work of other part-timers is specialized: Their skills are FedEx-specific, and they themselves must fit into the FedEx culture (or, as we shall see, cultures). As a result, the company sometimes calls on outside sources for part-time workers.

A GOOD PLACE TO BE— THOUGHTFUL AND IMAGINATIVE COMPENSATION SCHEMES

FedEx's concern for its employees permeates its human resources policies. The company feels particular responsibility for the families of its employees. It manifests that concern by providing flexibility in work hours, leaves-of-absence for family emergencies, and permanent part-time work.

Employees may structure their benefits packages to accommodate their age, health, career path, and other personal preferences. Tuition reimbursement is popular among package sorters, most of whom are young college students. Many thousands of college students have financed their educations through FedEx's benefits package.

More traditional benefits packages don't encompass the broad range of benefits FedEx offers. Most companies typically offer their employees a fairly standard package of vacation pay; health, life, and disability insurance; and wages and salaries dependent upon individual, department, and company performance.

FedEx has found that recognition for a specific job well done is often as important—and sometimes has more impact—than opportunities for promotion or compensation practices. It structures its reward programs to provide recognition as a main ingredient. Bravo Zulu, as we'll see in Chapter 3, rewards employees with free dinners, theater tickets, or $100 cash, at the manager's discretion. The company does not bestow its awards lightly. Everyone knows that to win such a tribute, an employee's performance must be extraordinary. The cash value of the trophy itself is modest, but the honor it bestows upon recipients is inestimable. Winners know that they are the Oscar winners of the express transportation business. They often forget the amount of the bonus, but they never forget when and why they get it. The "storytelling" that goes with such awards does much to create the mystique and reinforce culture at FedEx.

WHEN OPPORTUNITY KNOCKS, UNLOCK THE DOOR— CONTINUING EMPLOYEE-TRAINING PROGRAMS

Companies often miss the essential point of training. Give people opportunity—that's fine. But unless you also give them the power to make the most of it, you have perpetrated a fraud. And the power, of course, is in the training.

FedEx learned this lesson the hard way when it first experimented with self-managed teams about 10 years ago. "The first time we did a self-directed team it didn't work, and that was our fault," recalls Taylor. "It was in a central region, a small station out by itself....The employees in that work group were given no preparatory training. So it was not a success."

The next time the company established a self-directed team, "We wanted to make sure it was a success so we probably overtrained," Taylor says. "We put them through about nine months worth of training while they performed their own jobs. Everything from personnel management to engineering operations planning. That team has been a star group and has been the copy everyone has gone after...They have the lowest level of absenteeism, they have their prework meetings, they have their after-work meetings, they do all their vacation planning, all their scheduling, all workload balancing. They decide when they need to set up a temporary 'subteam.' They have a budget goal so they know what their cost per package should be....That group was the beginning of about 40 self-directed teams in the hub environment in every single region."

FedEx invests in its employees through a wide variety of ongoing training exercises. For example, new customer service agents must complete a six-week job-training program, and they must pass online job knowledge tests twice a year. Couriers have a similar program.

The human resources department establishes training standards, which include auditing the effectiveness of decentralized training programs for technical skill development. In addition to fostering job-specific abilities, FedEx training programs orient new hires to the corporate culture and provide instruction in such quality management methods as problem solving and process improvement. Line managers are responsible for insuring that all their employees are properly trained and can do their jobs. This requires directing them to appropriate training courses or interactive computerized instruction programs and working personally with them to develop their potential.

One of the most extensive corporate training programs is the company's Leadership Evaluation Awareness Process (LEAP). That program helps employees and the company determine whether management is the right path for them.

Once employees become senior managers, managing directors, or officers, they can take a variety of courses in the Leadership Institute to develop individual and team management skills. Outstanding FedEx senior managers and managing directors staff the Institute on a rotating basis. It promotes and teaches fundamental management precepts, with a uniquely FedEx perspective that enables managers to perfect skills the company most needs. For example, Institute courses include "Coaching for Commitment," "Exploring Teamwork," and "Participative Leadership."

An empowered workforce is one that has plenty of opportunity, along with the tools, skills, and backing to make the most of it. From the company's point of view, achievable opportunities are *responsibilities.*

ALL IN THE FEDEX FAMILY— A POLICY OF PROMOTION FROM WITHIN

The most attractive commitment is the FedEx promise, to all its people, of a real and open-ended future with the company. Promotion from within is not exactly a FedEx invention. Still, FedEx works at it. Managers who say they must go outside for a hire must prove it. And even when their credentials don't exactly match the job description, FedEx employees have the edge over outsiders. "Showing confidence in people tends to bring out their best, and they go the extra mile to grow into their responsibilities," says James Perkins. "Employees appreciate the company's commitment to them and their future," and their appreciation builds loyalty. Knowing they can get ahead without leaving FedEx is a powerful motivator of performance, and our customers also benefit from this policy."

What FedEx understands and acts on is something all employees know: A company, whether in the form of owners or shareholders, is investing its money in the enterprise; the employees are investing their lives. That should, and at FedEx it does, create a strong sense of responsibility.

FORGET GRIEVANCE PROCEDURES, SET UP JUSTICE PROCEDURES— THOROUGH DEDICATION TO PROCEDURAL FAIRNESS IN HANDLING GRIEVANCES

First, an anecdote from FedEx's *Manager's Pak*. An operations manager received a call from risk management that an accident had occurred in front of an office building that morning. The owner of the damaged vehicle was a building tenant and was informed of the accident by someone who witnessed the accident. The owner contacted the police who in turn notified FedEx's risk management. The manager called dispatch and asked that a general message be sent over a digitally assisted dispatch system (DADS), inquiring which courier from the station had made deliveries in the area that morning.

The manager determined that one of two couriers was involved. The DADS message was broadcast at approximately 1:30 p.m. At approximately 2:30 p.m. the courier at fault returned to the station and immediately notified the manager that he had hit a parked vehicle that morning. The employee stated that he "nosed" his van into the stop and, while backing out, he hit the parked car to his left. He got out of the van to note the damage to his van and the parked car. He further stated that he was extremely nervous about the accident and "panicked" because he did not want to have late deliveries in his Priority Overnight delivery cycle. The complainant admitted that he made a mistake by failing to immediately report his vehicle accident, but emphatically maintains that it was not his intention to withhold information concerning the accident and planned to report it when he returned to the station. The courier stated that he knew he made a mistake and was willing to accept any penalties.

When the manager reviewed the situation, he determined that the employee had waited some three hours before reporting the accident. By his own admission, the courier was nervous and drove away from the scene of the accident. The employee, who knew the policy on reporting vehicle accidents, did not leave a message on the parked vehicle, nor did he respond to the broadcast over DADS. The manager felt that he had no other choice but to terminate the employee based on his failure to immediately report the accident. Only after the DADS broadcast did the employee come forward.

Was there some other discipline necessary in this case? Did the employee's actions warrant total discharge?

The Appeals Board reviewed the documentation and investigative data regarding this case and it determined that the employee had not violated the actual letter of the policy. He did, in fact, report the accident to his manager immediately upon return to the station. It was not clear that the employee was attempting to cover up the accident. The employee was reinstated and issued a warning letter with a two-week disciplinary suspension to impress upon him the importance of immediately reporting any occurrence or accident to this manager.

In many organizations, nobody challenges management. But FedEx employees have recourse: the company's Guaranteed Fair Treatment Procedure. FedEx employees can take full advantage of that procedure.

Any FedEx employee who cannot resolve a dispute with a manager has the right to file a complaint that starts a three-step process up through the corporate hierarchy.

- **Step 1– Management Review Parties:** manager, senior manager, and managing director.

- **Step 2– Officer Review Parties:** vice president and senior vice president.

- **Step 3– Executive Review Parties:** CEO, executive vice president, chief personnel officer, and two senior vice presidents (rotating).

This widely praised, carefully fashioned "justice procedure" sends an unmistakable, and wonderfully morale-building, message to everyone in the company: You always have redress. The very existence of the procedure demonstrates that the company knows that injustices are done, and that managers, like other human beings, do them. Incidentally, this appeals process is a terrific way for the leadership of FedEx to keep a "pulse" on how employees are being treated by managers. In many companies, that truth is inadmissible: Hierarchy and authority must—at all costs—prevail. Not at FedEx.

LET EVERYBODY KNOW WHAT'S GOING ON— FREE, OPEN, TWO-WAY COMMUNICATION SYSTEMS

The afternoon before ABC's television show "20/20" criticized FedEx for its handling of hazardous materials, FedEx's own FXTV broke the story. On TV screens in every FedEx location employees watched executives talk about company policies for dealing with hazardous packages. As Fred Smith said at an AMA management briefing, the company believes in "going live as soon as possible after a major event or change to discuss the situation and open the phone lines to employees." FedEx shares bad news as well as good, and it's always willing to answer tough employee questions.

FXTV—a multimillion-dollar tool that provides instant contact between management and employees worldwide—exemplifies the company's approach to communication: quick, candid, comprehensive, and interactive. FXTV broadcasts daily news summaries, regular presentations of company goals and projects, and call-in programs on such topics as the previous night's service levels, what the competition is up to, and inclement weather that might affect the day's service. FXTV is a corporate CNN.

FedEx employs a staff of 50 in its employee communications department and spends about $70 per year per employee on print and audiovisual programs. The formal communications effort enhances and supports face-to-face manager-to-employee contact, which, surveys have found, is the way employees prefer to get information.

Just as important as providing information is management's willingness to listen. The chapter on communication in the FedEx *Manager's Guide* begins with a section called, "A FedEx Manager Must Be a Good Listener." It points out that, "listening as carefully and respectfully as possible reiterates as no other management action can that the employee is a valued member of our team."

The Open Door policy is one way FedEx listens. "The Open Door process is used by employees who feel that...existing policy is wrong and should be changed," Perkins explains. Employees send their questions or suggestions to the Open Door, which forwards it to the manager who has the authority and responsibility to make the changes.

The Best Practices program takes process improvements that employees suggest and makes them the new "standard practice."

ASK THE QUESTIONS, HEAR THE ANSWERS— KEEN ATTENTION TO EMPLOYEE OPINION

FedEx keeps its finger on the pulse of employee satisfaction through its annual survey of all U.S.-based employees. The Survey-Feedback-Action (SFA) questionnaire addresses universal employee concerns: fairness of pay levels, adequacy of the benefit program, how well work groups cooperate, and so forth. It also addresses issues that concern employees in the many individual FedEx locations scattered across the country.

Voluntary, anonymous participation in the survey approaches 100 percent. Employees know that their answers count. Each year the survey asks whether the company's responses to the concerns employees raised the year before have been satisfactory.

The human resources department compiles and analyzes employees' comments to determine both national and regional trends, and managers meet with their employees to review the findings. Most managers attend at least two feedback sessions: one presented to their employees, the other that their superiors conduct to discuss results of the survey and actions they'll initiate to address those results.

Employees rate their managers with such statements as, "My manager lets me know what's expected of me," "My manager treats me with respect and dignity," "Favoritism is a problem in my work group," "My manager is willing to listen to my concerns," and "My manager's boss does not give us the support we need." The assessments go either way.

Managers know that their SFA scores will affect their compensation. Therefore, they are eager to resolve budding problems before they take hold. For example, Steve Nielsen, who is now director of the company's Leadership Institute, recalls the time his employees complained that he showed favoritism when he made assignments. "I tried to explain that I rewarded the employees who seemed best qualified," he says. "After we discussed the facts, I realized I was making excuses for myself." Once he'd acknowledged the problem, Nielsen worked with his group to correct it. The group now tracks every request for an assignment, and the new assignment-rotation system accommodates any interested employee. With the new system in place, employees feel more involved and satisfied in their work process.

Occasionally a problem's solution concerns only one particular work group, but most remedial actions are company-wide. For example, should a survey uncover safety problems in some work groups, the safety department might very well respond with new procedures, equipment, and training throughout the organization. One recent survey revealed that employees felt the company's communication on goals and objectives was inadequate. In response, Fred Smith decided to answer employees' questions himself on a quarterly FXTV call-in show.

Fred Smith gave FedEx a head start by building people-oriented policies into his organization right from the beginning. While its commitment to employees has been constant, FedEx didn't deliver today's workplace overnight. The environment evolves day by day and decision by decision.

How can managers in other organizations give power and parity to their employees? FedEx's human-resource techniques provide a dynamic model:

Establish A Formal Goal. Put employees first. Create mechanisms for measuring progress. Tom Peters has observed that you get what you measure. To change human or organizational behavior set a clear objective, decide what success will look like, and track progress toward it. Not every company wants to place employee goals on a par with service and profits. You must determine what you want to achieve and how you will measure your performance. Then, establish a time frame, the steps you'll take, and the human and dollar resources you'll commit.

It's difficult to quantify the competitive benefits of putting people first, but FedEx's top managers believe it was the dominant contributing factor to its winning the Malcolm Baldrige National

Quality Award in 1994. They believe it underlies FedEx's excellent customer satisfaction ratings.

Check the Alignment of Your Goals and Your Culture, and Make Adjustments. To reach your destination, your human and organizational behavior must be in line with your company's objectives.

All the FedEx rewards programs align with People-Service-Profit goals. Some link directly to annual, measurable business goals, and others promote and reinforce employee behavior that creates value for the company. Taylor says, "Our employees recognize that they truly do get rewards for results. It's not just the amount of effort that goes into something; it's producing a result."

Find Out What Employees and Managers Want, Need, and Have to Offer. Respond in kind. That is critical. While many organizations survey their employees and ask for employee suggestions, few react productively. Before you begin two-way communication with your employees, have a plan for analyzing and responding to the information you receive. Failing to do that sends a loud, ugly message: Management doesn't care. Make sure you focus your surveys on factors you want to address. Don't ask a question if you're not prepared to deal with the answer.

Commit to the Long Haul. It takes time to build an organization that, like Federal Express, values and empowers employees. Change may be gradual, so employees and managers must see that the company is taking coherent, meaningful steps.

When Things Go Wrong, Your Employees Should Not Pay for Management's Mistakes. In 1992, FedEx withdrew from domestic service within Europe and shifted focus to the intercontinental business. It meant that more than 6,500 Europe employees were laid off. Says senior vice president for global sales and trade services, David Rebholz, "we were diligent. We could have said, 'Oh yeah, well, that's Europe.' We could have done that, but we tried to help find new jobs for our European employees with other companies in Europe." When the company expanded in Europe a few years later, people already knew FedEx as an excellent employer, one for whom they would happily work.

Treat All Employees Like Customers. Everyone in an organization has customers—both internal and external—and everyone is a customer of others who work in a process. FedEx feels that the principles that create loyal external customers also create loyal internal customers—the employees.

Give Employees the Opportunity to Serve Customers, and Make Sure Your Procedures Don't Impede Them. Don't let rules become substitutes for thinking. Employees who go beyond their job descriptions to provide service to their customers create inestimable value, customer satisfaction, and financial success. Find out what motivates certain employees to go the extra mile while others do only what it takes to get by.

Use the Right Rewards to Generate Extra Effort. FedEx's wide-ranging reward and incentive programs motivate sales, service, management, and project performance.

Reward Everyone Who Introduces Notable and Effective Improvements. When a new manager took over a group of poorly performing sales engineers, he made a dramatic difference with a combination of recognition, respect, and perks.

Make Sure Everybody in Your Company Knows How to Earn Rewards. Unlike companies that keep bonuses a deep, dark secret, FedEx encourages winners to talk about them. Corporate communication vehicles like FXTV and newsletters are full of winners' stories. Talking about rewards helps everybody understand what makes a winner.

....

A CHECKLIST FOR MANAGERS

Does your company put people first? If you, like FedEx managers, can answer yes to the following questions, you and your employees are in good shape.

1. Does your organization have policies and practices designed to minimize or avoid layoffs?

2. Is there a mechanism to hear employee grievances and concerns? Is it fair? Do your employees believe it is fair? Can employees take their grievances all the way to the CEO, if necessary?

3. Are top managers committed to employee-friendly policies? Do their actions demonstrate true commitment? Can you describe three events from the past 12 months that illustrate such commitment?

4. Do your policies and practices protect worker safety? What have you done in the past 12 months that demonstrates your concern for your employees' health and safety?

5. Does your company regularly survey employees to keep abreast of their needs? Is there a mechanism for acting on the concerns you identify? Do you get follow-up feedback to see if employees agree there is improvement?

6. Does your company customize policies and benefits to suit different employee groups?

7. Do your employees review the performance of their managers? Do their reviews have an impact on the managers' compensation?

8. Is there a clear connection between performance and your reward-and-recognition policies? Do employees understand and credit the connection?

9. Does your company make a sincere and ongoing effort to promote from within?

10. Are your corporate communications clear, candid, and regular? Is there a mechanism for soliciting and responding to employee feedback and ideas?

11. Do the company's goals promote and enable performance at all levels? Give three examples—from different levels of your organization—that demonstrate how the company's goals promote and enable your employees' performance.

12. Do managers and employees receive the training they need to excel at their jobs?

13. Do employees make decisions that affect company procedures and policies? Looking back over the past 12 months, can you recall three such decisions and your employees' contributions to those decisions?

14. Do your managers have specific responsibility for coaching and supporting workers?

CHAPTER 2

Everybody Pitches In

....

Does your company value fluid, cross-functional teamwork? Do those values emanate from the top— from the CEO and other senior executives?

Does everyone in your company understand and strive to further its vision of what it's doing in the world?

Are there company anecdotes you could tell a stranger to illustrate your commitment to unconstrained cooperation? To unconstrained thinking? In your own work group? In other work groups?

....

Four words spark dread in the hearts of customers, managers, and anyone else trying to get something done: "It's not my job." That phrase sums up a mentality that management in the United States and Europe has spent decades trying to combat. Hammer and Champy, in *Reengineering the Corporation,* have written about the reengineered, or "boundaryless," corporation where "silos" or "boxes" don't constrain employees' performance.

Well, to put the matter bluntly, there are no silos at Federal Express Corporation. Nor are there boxes. Of course, every employee at FedEx has specified duties and responsibilities. At the same time, though, every employee has the duty and responsibility to help out wherever and whenever help is needed. This everyone-pitches-in attitude permeates the company. If couriers fall behind on their appointed rounds, there are always others who will take time to help. No one has to tell them to help, they simply do. Such cooperation and collaboration are as much a part of the FedEx spirit as its commitment to timeliness.

The basic principle is that every FedEx employee—courier, sorter, pilot, public relations specialist—learns to focus on what really counts: the customer. Managers at every level, including senior vice presidents, make sales calls and, when needed, load packages in the hubs. At the FedEx-sponsored Orange Bowl, employees will entertain customers and demonstrate new products and technologies. Everywhere, at all times, whatever their rank or function, FedEx people work together to achieve the common goal: the all-important FedEx guarantee.

What's behind the FedEx everyone-pitches-in ethos? A leader who is a boundary buster; departmental boundaries that are meant to be crossed; the ability to discern fine detail while considering the larger context—that is to say, forest-and-trees thinking; employees as salespeople; and customers who pitch in, too.

TAKING IT FROM THE TOP— A LEADER WHO IS A BOUNDARY BUSTER

Company-wide benefits emerge when employees from different sectors of the organization team together. Say, for example, FedEx has a problem related to high costs of sorting. It forms a team: a sort worker, an industrial engineer, an information system supervisor, a courier, a traffic clerk, and a quality engineer. All of those employees contribute from their individual perspectives.

The sort worker describes the problem from the operational perspective; the industrial engineer talks about the costs of the operation; the information system supervisor says that she can design a report that will help them analyze the problem and track results after they implement improvements; the quality engineer says he knows how to devise a technique to drive down costs, and so forth. One idea builds on another. The team members work together, crossing lines, making suggestions, agreeing on solutions. But the first, absolute prerequisite is that everyone works in an open, cooperative learning environment.

Fred Smith has long believed that ideas and solutions to problems don't recognize departmental boundaries or job descriptions. Everyone is potentially the person who will penetrate the impenetrable.

Fog is FedEx's great mischief-maker: It delays flights, spreads anxiety, and costs the company the pure gold of *time*. "Since the invention of the airplane," Smith told *Inc.* magazine, "people have been looking for a way to fly through fog. And the solutions all went in the direction of creating systems that eliminated the need for the pilot to see, in favor of machines that 'see.' As a result, you now have these very complex systems that bring planes in using lots of on-the-ground electronic equipment, and the damn things are always breaking down.

"So we kept looking at the problem. We even went to Paris to look at big machines that blew fog off the runways there. They cost $12 million apiece. Not right.

"Then, one day I was on a plane with a bright guy who worked for us, Charles Brandon, and he was reading a magazine article about the Air Force using millimeter-wave radar to take pictures through the clouds. And all of a sudden Charles looked at me and said, 'You know, what we ought to do is try to see through the fog.' In other words, put the pilot back in the loop, which was 180 degrees from what everyone else had done. Well, to make a long story short, it's absolutely feasible to see through fog."

The point of such anecdotes is not simply that Smith establishes the model of the company's boundary-busting thinking. His example sends another powerful message: FedEx is a company where ideas are not precious stones, which lonely prospectors mine, hoard, and surreptitiously trade for cash. At FedEx, good ideas are certainly precious, and they earn generous rewards. Fresh air and revitalizing breezes rather than diamonds and rubies are the guiding metaphors. Ideas are the essential components of the atmosphere.

BOUNDARY BUSTING CAN AND SHOULD BE INTERNATIONAL

For an example of how everyone pitches in, let's consider events that had important consequences for the company. In the early 1990s, FedEx set out to establish a superhub site to service Asia. Joe McCarty—the senior vice president then in charge of Asia and the Pacific—had the mission of finding the right location.

McCarty was considering several sites when the Philippines' Subic Bay Metropolitan Authority approached him. Subic Bay, an inlet of the South China Sea off Luzon in the Philippines, had provided a base for the U.S. Navy for many years. With hangars to accommodate FedEx's sorting operations, large concrete aprons capable of handling planeside sorts, and millions of square feet of warehouse space, it was a natural choice for a major hub. Like the SuperHub in Memphis, Subic Bay even had its own power system.

After looking over the site, McCarty met with Filipino President Fidel V. Ramos and his ministers. After a few months of negotiation, they reached an agreement. However, a new problem confronted McCarty. Japan, fearing the effect of an Asian FedEx presence on its own transportation industry, refused FedEx permission to service the Japanese market from Subic Bay. Given Japan's reputation for stubborn protectionism, that totally unexpected twist might have overcome the commitment of a less resourceful company. Instead, to break down the Japanese barrier and get the business rolling in Asia, FedEx mobilized talent from every quarter of the company.

In many companies, McCarty's problem would have remained McCarty's problem. He would have struggled along for a while, relying on his own resources. Eventually, perhaps, he might have begged for assistance from other departments. But the other departments would have had no vested interest in helping him, and their employees would have had to get approval—and direction—from their own managers. FedEx, however, is not that kind of a company. At FedEx, departmental boundaries are meant to be crossed.

In the United States, Ken Masterson, FedEx's chief legal counsel, teamed with Doyle Cloud, vice president of government affairs, to get the support of the U.S. Congress and the departments of State and Transportation. Government-to-government negotiations dragged on and on, but FedEx wasn't waiting patiently. With McCarty leading the charge, FedEx mounted a daring and extensive public relations campaign in Japan itself.

McCarty aimed to convince Japanese executives that an agreement would help their businesses. He enlisted a small army of FedEx employees to analyze issues, conduct market research on the Japanese transportation industry, prepare briefs, write speeches, and design ways to win hearts and minds. The campaign reached its peak on July 5, 1995, when, in one day, after speaking before the Transportation Club in Tokyo, the transport reporters, and the Foreign Correspondence Club of Japan, McCarty made an appearance on Japanese television. Gradually, the Japanese perception of FedEx—an avaricious American company that planned to crush the smaller Japanese transportation companies— evolved to a picture of a good citizen of Japan, albeit a foreign one with headquarters in the United States. The Japanese were convinced, too, that FedEx would add services to their market and help it grow, creating a bigger pie for all transportation companies in Japan. For FedEx, the campaign has set the standard for team performance: Many employees pitched in—going far beyond the boundaries of their jobs—to accomplish the impossible. People who don't normally collaborate in the course of their day-to-day duties experience noteworthy results when they get together on projects. Here's how I think of it: proximity increases productivity. Not incidentally, it was a winning performance. The Japanese accepted FedEx's schedule request to connect Subic Bay and Japan.

REMEMBERING WHAT BUSINESS YOU'RE IN— FOREST-AND-TREES THINKING

In the Middle Ages, an ancient story goes, a merchant came upon an old man cutting limestone in a quarry. "What are you doing?" asked the merchant. "Why, I'm building a cathedral," the old man replied, as if it were completely obvious. FedEx employees see their jobs in terms that define both their day-to-day responsibilities and the goals of the company.

FedEx calls this forest-and-trees thinking: People are mindful of details, but their concern for detail doesn't distract them from the larger picture. Suppose the old quarry worker had needed the merchant's help cutting his limestone: What would have done more to move the passerby to help? The thought that he would be cutting limestone or the thought that he would be building a cathedral, or a castle, or even, for that matter, a barn? The answer is clear.

But how do you keep the forest—or the cathedral—continually in focus? One way is to encourage systems thinking. The FedEx *Manager's Guide* says people must recognize "patterns affecting reality and...how to change or influence them effectively. It is the art of seeing 'both the forest and the trees,' producing effective change along with an awareness of the consequences that change will have on the whole organization....In our culture where change seems to occur at a fast pace, organizations have an optimum rate of growth."

GETTING NEW BUSINESS IS EVERYONE'S BUSINESS—EMPLOYEES AS SALESPEOPLE

The company-wide understanding that everyone markets FedEx services to customers is the most apparent manifestation of the everyone-pitches-in ethos. At FedEx, hands-on experience begins with senior management. Each corporate officer has a sales territory where he or she routinely makes calls. Jim Perkins, senior vice president of human resources, finds that involvement truly compelling. "It's a tremendous experience," he said. "There is nothing comparable to being face-to-face with customers. You quickly understand their needs. You know when you're not meeting their expectations. And you learn that their expectations are never unreasonable, because their environments are always changing. What may have been an unthinkable service expectation on the part of a customer today will be routine in tomorrow's competitive environment."

Perkins recalls a visit he made to one of the TV networks. "We were trying to get all of its business," he said. "You know, some customers have internal problems you must identify and help them with before they give you the business. This particular customer was very concerned about billing allocations within the various departments of his firm. It was an internal problem, but we were able to provide systems help for the firm, and we got the order."

Perkins enjoys stepping out into the sales world. "It's always nice to see the people who are paying the bills....It has a leveling effect on your perspective and keeps your head in the business."

At FedEx, employees are continually on the lookout for new customers, more people to pay the bills. The company rewards sales leads from people at every level of its organization. That program calls for employees to submit the names of potential customers to the sales department. If the sales department converts those prospects to customers, the referring employees earn extra compensation. The program is particularly effective in a company such as FedEx where large numbers of employees have contact with the market. It's built-in market research in action.

GOING TO THE SOURCE— CUSTOMERS THAT PITCH IN, TOO

Customers have the best vantage point when it comes to the services they need. That's a cliché of today's management wisdom. *How* you tap into that lode of information makes a big difference. Most companies collect information customer by customer. FedEx does that. It also does much more. Regularly—formally and informally—the company assembles customers to glean their insights, opinions, and reactions to new and existing FedEx services.

The Orange Bowl, which FedEx sponsors, is a case in point. The company invites customers from around the world to attend the festivities and participate in meetings.

For each Orange Bowl, FedEx rents a centrally located hotel and arranges plenty of entertainment, sightseeing, cocktail parties, and fancy dinners. Product displays surround customers, and there are FedEx managers on the scene to answer customers' questions. Over the several days surrounding the main event, customers wander through the displays, commenting about them and chatting among themselves and with FedEx personnel about service. The mix of people is synergistic. One customer puts out an idea he has had, another joins in with her version of how that idea would appeal to her. It doesn't take long before the group has molded a pretty thoughtful and valuable concept.

FedEx has its best and brightest managers at the Orange Bowl, listening to what their customers are saying, taking notes, encouraging analyses of the services, probing for comments, complaints, and problems.

During such events the company both entertains its customers and earns their goodwill. An important by-product is that FedEx gathers the best market research available. And, like so much else FedEx does, the benefit is not limited to the marketing professionals. Managers from every other sector of the company learn the customer's perspective as well. At FedEx, all employees must know what pleases customers, what turns them off, and how to correct their problems.

Creating an organization where employees feel free to pitch in, cross boundaries, and contribute their ideas for improvement is a demanding task. For some large older corporations, it's probably impossible. Fred Smith was relatively fortunate: he had started with a fresh, new organization. He could mold and shape the company's policies to accelerate change.

Even if your company is older and set in its ways, it still can be done. Yes, it's harder to make changes, but you have to start somewhere.

Here are some steps you can take to smooth your company's transformation into one where everyone pitches in:

Create an Atmosphere in Which Any Employee Can Advance an Idea That Adds Value to the Company—Beyond That Employee's Organizational Unit. I work with the University of Memphis as the first Federal Express Professor of Excellence in the Fogelman College of Business. I proposed and developed the university's Center for Cycle Time Research, which provides diagnostic services and prescriptive solutions to the logistical challenges—from inventory management to delivery schedules—that confront FedEx customers.

My grant doesn't pay for me simply to work with the university. My goal is to create new paradigms for academia's and industry's pooling their efforts to improve business processes. I am working also to extend the impact of my research program internationally.

Develop Company Policies That Not Only Permit, But Encourage Boundary-Busting Behavior. First and foremost, you'll need to train your employees. The everyone-pitches-in ideal will yield limited rewards for the company if employees don't have the skills to do the job. The payoff for the company grows in direct proportion to the skill level of your employees.

Construct and Publicize Models of Behavior and Expectations for All Jobs. I'm not talking about job descriptions: You need flexible job explanations that allow your employees to cross departmental lines and think creatively beyond their particular jobs' boundaries.

Develop an Environment of Trust and Cooperative Learning. The FedEx environment, for instance, permits couriers to learn from customer service representatives and both groups learn from inventory control specialists. Every employee knows certain things and has certain skills that other employees don't share. When they learn from one another, employees have the opportunity to see, observe, and discover what other employees do well, and they absorb that knowledge and apply what works to their own jobs. All employees have opportunities to grow and broaden their performance capabilities.

It's often hard to get employees to open up to one another, particularly if they work in a company that doesn't readily accept ideas, and most particularly—in functionally oriented companies—to people in other departments. In some companies, managers hesitate to let their counterparts in other departments know what they do: They fear such frankness could reduce their value. In such organizations there is no mutual trust. Companies need to tear down the "Berlin walls" that separate coworkers, and the way to do that is by recognizing and rewarding cooperative behavior. It may take some time, but the effort is worth it.

When Employees Have the Courage to Admit They Don't Know Something, They Enhance the Cooperative Learning Environment. In a closed organization, where everybody suspects everybody else, most employees are reluctant to admit they don't know everything: It's looked on as a mark of weakness.

You'll know you've succeeded when employees voluntarily own up to their mistakes and acknowledge that they're not satisfied with certain aspects of their own performance and the extent of their knowledge; they realize they can speak without fear of reprisal; and they recognize that their ignorance is not unique. Everybody is born ignorant and spends life suffering from that malady. If you can help people overcome the feelings of mistrust that accompany ignorance, you can certainly accomplish much more.

In the End, What You're Doing Is Telling Employees You Value Their Ideas. Encourage them to advance ideas in a no-risk atmosphere. Provide the training they need. Create a cooperative environment where everyone learns from everyone else. Then measure results, publicize successes, and reward the employees behind the successes.

....

A CHECKLIST FOR MANAGERS

Does the intricacy of your company's workings stymie your employees' enthusiasm? To find out whether your company and employees are contributing the best of their talents and abilities, take this test.

1. Does your company value fluid, cross-functional teamwork? Do those values emanate from the top—from the CEO and the other executives?

2. Are there programs that encourage people to pitch in and help one another wherever they're needed?

3. Does everyone in your company understand and strive to further the vision of what it's doing in the world?

4. Are there systems, practices, and rituals in place that inculcate that vision? Can you describe them to a stranger?

5. Does your company value broad, free-ranging thinking? From everyone?

6. Are there clear, unmistakable opportunities for such thinking? Inducements? Rewards?

7. Are there company anecdotes you could relate to a new hire that illustrate your commitment to unconstrained cooperation? To unconstrained thinking?

8. Do your managers set an example of trust and openness among themselves and with all other employees? Describe an instance of such trust and openness in a situation that called for facing unpleasant facts or mistakes?

9. Are there opportunities for everyone in your company to meet and learn from customers?

CHAPTER 3

Rewards Are Absolutely, Positively Everything

....

Does your compensation program reflect your employees' contributions to your company's success?

Has your company developed a way to track all aspects of performance including, among other factors, leadership, customer service, and profitability?

Do your employees value the rewards superior performance brings? Does everyone, for example, prefer money? Do you allow "different strokes for different folks"?

How often do you bestow rewards? Do you present awards spontaneously, or do people know that there are only specified times when they can hope to gain recognition for their efforts?

....

Look back at Chapter 1—"You Can Never, Ever, Do Enough for Your People." Remember FedEx's sincere, all-out commitment to job security? Well, I hope there's been no misunderstanding—the company's people-first policy does not entail tenure. FedEx is as ready as the next outfit to fire incompetent workers and managers.

Nevertheless, at FedEx the main motivator is the carrot, not the stick. Indeed, make that carrots, plural. FedEx has a long shelf full of incentives to greater effort, greater creativity, and greater care. Reasonable job security is one aspect of FedEx's remarkable environment of opportunity. Promotion from within is another. The third is a palpable concern for the particular needs of individual employees. The fourth is a flexible and imaginative benefits package. We discussed all four in Chapter 1. The fifth—and perhaps for most readers the most important—is compensation. FedEx has established a system of compensation that really makes a difference to its employees' contentment while reinforcing their loyalty. How? FedEx's rewards work: The rewards link directly to performance, and people value them.

TURNING EVERYONE'S EYES TO THE PRIZES— REWARDS THAT WORK

It's a tricky matter, setting up a scheme of incentives to get the best—in fact, better and better—work out of your employees. Sure, you can conduct performance reviews, and, every six months or so, when John and Mary come for your assessments, you can stand them under a warm shower of praise. But what about the long haul? What happens to John's and Mary's motivations after the glow of the performance review has faded? What happens, for that matter, when the shower is cold?

Among American employers, FedEx's compensation policies are exemplary. It's not that FedEx employees earn fatter paychecks: Their pay is competitive with pay for comparable positions at other companies. What makes FedEx's compensation policies noteworthy is the imagination and care that supports their design and administration. Bonuses, commissions, rewards, prizes, peer recognition, and incentives—all of those and more combine to produce a many-faceted reward system that encourages employees to work at peak performance.

According to Tracy Schmidt, senior vice president for air ground terminals and transportation, "We are moving increasingly toward performance-based reward systems. We want to align our employees' compensation with their fulfilling goals that are congruent with the company's. Not every employee agrees with this approach, but it is crucial to remaining competitive." Translated, that means that FedEx stresses pay for performance; pay for solid, practical, and implemented ideas; and pay for outstanding customer service. Whether as individuals or as members of teams and groups, FedEx employees who know how to improve quality, productivity, and customer satisfaction benefit directly, and sometimes instantly, from their contributions. Moreover, while FedEx is careful to establish realistic, attainable goals, it also makes sure that the goals aren't *too* easily attainable. It wants its people to stretch a bit. Compensation and rewards, FedEx knows, are part of a company's "justice system," but they are also, emphatically, instruments of productivity growth.

FedEx designed its rewards on the same principle of mass customization that guides its customer services. Different contributions win different rewards. These are the major ones:

- Bravo Zulu awards, as described by the *Manager's Guide,* are "visible recognition for 'above and beyond' performance....In the U.S. Navy, the Bravo and Zulu flags indicate, 'well done.'" Such instant recognition is useful in any organization, particularly one that relies on teamwork and cooperation as much as FedEx does. Those discretionary awards can be cash, dinner with or without the boss, theater tickets, or any other reward that stresses recognition for a job well done. Recently, for example, a quality team went far beyond the call of duty in their investigation of persistent customer complaints: Team members visited many FedEx district locations, trained staff who needed to improve their skills, and provided checklists that help identify and prevent recurring complaints. As a result, such complaints dropped by 20 to 50 percent. A New York FedEx courier won an individual Bravo Zulu for "above and beyond" resourcefulness. When his van died in the middle of his route, he loaded up his hand truck and raced on foot to complete most of his deliveries. After delivering those packages he could, he realized that certain 10:30 a.m. deliveries were in jeopardy. He did the impossible: The courier hailed a cab at the height of the rush hour and delivered every package—on time.

- Finder's Keepers awards extra cash to FedEx couriers, customer service representatives, and other employees who have daily contact with customers, for new customers they bring in. "I just looked at my list of October winners," Mary Alice Taylor recently told me. "We have people who have added as much as $1,300 to their monthly pay. Finder's Keepers has generated $120 million of new business for the company thus far."

- Best Practice Pays is a team cash award, which many FedEx employees can win when their output and contributions exceed company-set goals. These rewards recognize operational improvements.

- Golden Falcon Awards go to employees whom customers and management have nominated for recognition. Many Golden Falcons grace the mantels of couriers and other employees who have come to the aid of people in distress. FedEx operations manager Frank Anthamatten delivered essential medicine to two young boys during the 1994 Georgia floods. The boys depend on an intravenous medical supplement for nourishment. FedEx routinely delivers the weekly supplements directly to their home, but during the flood all routes were officially closed. Anthamatten, ignoring the danger, drove five and a half torturous hours on flooded roads, finally delivering the medication at 3:00 a.m. The boys' nurse reported Anthamatten's dedication, and the company awarded him the Golden Falcon.

- Five Star Awards For Leadership recognize outstanding performance by individual contributors who, during the course of the year, make truly significant contributions toward attaining the company's objectives. Managers prize the rewards because everyone knows that FedEx does not hand out Five Stars lightly. Award-winning contributions are always exceptional achievements like doubling budgeted sales or starting a major new project for the company. James Perkins, for example, won the Five Star Award for his development of an innovative health care plan that maintained a high level of employee service while significantly reducing health care and workers' compensation costs.

- Star/SuperStar awards recognize the organization's best performers with checks worth 2 to 3 percent of their salary. Those checks supplement money and stock they receive through performance reviews and merit increases.

MAKING ACHIEVEMENT COUNT— REWARDS WITH A DIRECT LINK TO PERFORMANCE

FedEx, as you can see, ties rewards to performance. That is not an uncommon state of affairs, in business or anywhere else. Rewards by their nature are given for performance and achievement. Still, in business—as opposed, say, to sports—giving rewards is not so straightforward: How do you measure performance? Measurement doesn't present much of a problem when it comes to contributions to the bottom line, or even outstanding delivery efforts in New York City and extraordinary heroism on the flooded back roads of Georgia. But how do you measure such elusive qualities as "leadership" and certain nebulous aspects of "service"? The answer is, of course: As best you can. And FedEx does it very well indeed.

Human resources chief James Perkins says, "Look at People-Service-Profit. We actually measure all three: We measure the people side of the house, the service side of the house, and the profit side of the house." The company has defined key elements and how to measure them within each of those categories.

With regard to People, for instance, FedEx looks closely at the company's leaders and whether they create environments in which employees can prosper. The company has exhaustively analyzed leadership qualities. As Perkins says, "What we did was to study certain leaders who through reputation, achievements, performance appraisals, and the like were considered to be excellent performers within the organization. We talked with their bosses, peers, and subordinates and distilled the characteristics and qualities of what constitutes leadership at FedEx.

"Then," he continues, "we incorporated these criteria into a screening program that we call LEAP (Leadership Evaluation and Awareness Process). It is a program that all FedEx management people must go through prior to being certified to lead." But that's not the end of it. FedEx measures the quality of its people's leadership on an ongoing basis. The first ten questions on the Survey Feedback Action (SFA), Perkins explains, deal with leadership. My employees answer questions about my performance. 'My boss,' for example, 'keeps me informed; he tells me when I have done a good job.' All of my subordinates rate me." But tracking this information is also useful for measuring the stuff FedEx is made of. Perkins concludes, "It's one of our strengths."

FedEx measures the service portion of People-Service-Profits through its Service Quality Indicator (SQI). The SQI is a sophisticated tool that measures how well FedEx satisfies its customers. Since its inception in 1987, it has brought about major improvements to customer service levels. For a more complete description of FedEx's Service Quality Indicator process, see Chapter 11.

The third leg of the People-Service-Profits triangle is profits. FedEx produces the usual array of financial statements to measure financial results. During the budgeting process the company determines its pretax goals for the coming fiscal year. It develops financial budgets down to the lowest possible organizational component. Supervisors and teams have access to all the financial data they need to manage their functions. Management expects them to use the numbers to keep their own segments of the organization in tune with the budget.

At FedEx, in short, performance measurement systems reinforce the company's mission and objectives. Everything works together: objectives to measurements; measurements to performance; performance to rewards.

PROMISING (AND DELIVERING) WHAT THEY WANT—REWARDS THAT PEOPLE VALUE

Many people are astonished by the vast array of FedEx's rewards. It's simply not effective to present identical rewards to everyone: After all, what excites you may leave me flat. Maybe what keeps you motivated is a nice fat bonus check every quarter. I might prefer to be assigned to a critical, highly visible project. It's important to remember that a system of rewards must be broad enough to accommodate as many tastes as possible.

Recently, as part of the Cycle Time research program, we provided FedEx a new software tool called Motivator™. It helps managers identify and customize rewards to individual employees. The philosophy behind such a tool: Do unto others as they want done unto them.

Let's say I tell you that if you sell 100,000 widgets for our company, you will receive a cash bonus of $25,000. Two events must occur for this reward to be meaningful to you. First, you must believe that selling 100,000 widgets is possible. Then you must feel that the reward of $25,000 is worth working for. If you do not believe selling 100,000 widgets is doable, or if you think the effort is worth $50,000, not the $25,000 I have promised you, your motivation won't be strong enough. If you think you can sell 100,000 widgets but you would much prefer five weeks vacation in Hawaii to the $25,000, you may not try as hard to achieve the sales goal.

As your supervisor, I must discover what reward you truly value. And I must continue to reexamine your desires because what motivates you today may not do the trick tomorrow. Unlike your personality or your work style, reward goals change. If, the next year, you become a parent, what you may truly value then is a cash bonus so you can build an addition to your house.

There is another important aspect to rewards that many companies miss. In more traditional companies employee recognition begins and ends at the annual performance review. Often, however, the process results in a performance drop-off.

Most organizations distribute rewards in one of two common ways. Probably the larger portion of employers schedule reviews at specific intervals, annually or, perhaps, semiannually. There's a problem with that approach, though. The intervals between rewards are quite long, and the long-awaited rewards often cause an unfortunate roller-coaster effect. When the time approaches for employees' reviews, the level of their effort climbs considerably only to fall precipitously right after their evaluations. Many parents will recognize that as Christmas behavior. As the holiday approaches, kids' behavior is exemplary, but, in the days following, too often, parents note disappointing recidivism.

To avoid that up-and-down effect, some employers try to maintain a regimen of continuous reinforcement. The employers define their expectations very clearly, and when their people perform according to those instructions and accomplish the goals management has articulated, management praises and acknowledges the productivity. Problems develop, however, when management decides, after a period of offering such encouraging remarks, that the employees are trained to the point of needing no more reinforcement. The employees, for their part, react badly to the lack of recognition. If you asked one of them, he or she might say, "You certainly appreciated my work when I first started, but now you don't, and you take me and my contributions for granted." Sometimes, in order to meet the goals their supervisors set, employees might have to work late or even over the weekend. If management fails to acknowledge or reward their extraordinary contributions until their scheduled review—six months or even a year later—they may likely feel that, "It's not worth the effort." Of course the first time the employee fails to deliver, the unhappy supervisor may resort even to punishment.

The strategy of continuous reinforcement is perilous because it's so difficult to sustain. Unless you can uphold that encouraging mode, it's ultimately a bad strategy: Most of us can't remember to keep up the effort.

Recognizing the limitations of both periodic, and continuous reinforcement, FedEx has found that the best response is to reward top performance on a random, rather than only on a fixed basis. Look at it this way: You expect a gift on your birthday. You expect a gift on your anniversary. You expect a gift at Christmas. If you don't receive those gifts, you're disappointed. But gifts given out of the blue are the ones that have the most impact. Similarly, in a work situation, unscheduled recognition is especially memorable. To bring my point to life, I often ask people in my seminars whether they have ever received a salary increase outside the standard review process. I generally get a response rate of less than 3 percent, yet each of those people remembers vividly where and when it happened.

FedEx institutionalizes its system of spontaneous rewards through its many well-publicized programs. Its mass customization program provides employees with rewards that are valuable to them individually. Providing flexible rewards on spontaneous occasions, FedEx fosters an environment that stimulates excellent performance.

FedEx has a very special rewards program. Here are some of its design principles, which you can adapt for your own company:

Tie Compensation to Performance. By that, I don't mean to say that employees should get paid only after they accomplish a given amount of work. Most full-time FedEx employees are paid hourly, as are part-timers. The reward program provides further compensation and recognition for outstanding performers. The crucial feature of FedEx remuneration is that employees earn rewards based on their contributions, rather than on the time they spend on the job.

Develop a Series Of Measurements That Form an Objective Base for Determining Eligibility for Rewards. It should have three components: (1) managerial effectiveness or, as FedEx calls it, leadership, (2) customer service, and (3) profits. Establish specific measurements for all three categories. While most companies understand financial reports (profit and loss, balance sheets, cash flow, operating variances, and the like), they often exclude important measurements of customer and employee satisfaction.

Measure, too, how well each level of the company is performing relative to corporate objectives. That step helps to make sure that all employees march to the beat of the same drummer. If, for example, one of your corporate objectives is to reduce quality costs by 20 percent in the upcoming fiscal year, all employees should know what they need to do to help attain that goal.

Rewards Must Be Valuable to Their Recipients. If Janet likes to dine out, pay for her dinner at a top restaurant. If Peter prefers cash, cut him a check. Most human resource departments seem to have a bias toward cash rewards. That's a remnant of the 1960s when companies considered cash the prime motivator.

Do Not Grant Rewards Only at Fixed Intervals. It's fine to conduct performance reviews. But it's not okay simply to throw Janet a 5 percent increase at her performance review, pat her on the back for a job well done, and forget about her until next year. That's a sure way to encourage employee efforts to lag. Naturally, there are always some employees who are self-motivated. But they are few and rare. Most employees need the continual reinforcement that signals approval of performance. That's why the FedEx approach of allowing random rewards raises the expectations of employees. To satisfy your own personal sense of organization, you might devise a schedule for your reward-giving days by going through your calendar, selecting days at random, and entering reminders that will prompt you to recognize deserving employees. On those dates, take the time to talk to employees whose outstanding work you appreciate. And be sure to give each one the reward that he or she will remember.

Develop a Selection of Rewards Appropriate for Different Jobs and Levels of Performance. The value of a reward should reflect the value of improvement. Too many managers impose a cap on rewards—a piddling amount of cash that has the unintended impact of an insult—even though some ideas generate literally hundreds of thousands of dollars in cost savings or sales.

Be Sure That Your Reward Program Recognizes Leadership Ability and Customer Service—The People and Service Legs of the People-Service-Profits Triangle. Develop specific programs so your employees don't concentrate only on costs and profits. A single-minded focus on profits produces employees who ignore customers' concerns. Supervisors and managers who center their attentions almost exclusively on profits forget their leadership responsibilities. That lessens the we're-all-in-this-together philosophy, and it can deteriorate into, "Every man (woman) for himself (herself)!"

A CHECKLIST FOR MANAGERS

Are you confident that your compensation programs are having the desired impact? Here are a few questions you ought to consider:

1. Does your compensation program reflect your employees' contributions to your company's success?

2. Contributions can range across a wide spectrum: from generating increases in sales to reducing wastes in the production line. Do you acknowledge all of them?

3. Has your company developed a way to track all aspects of performance, including, among other factors, leadership, customer service, and profitability?

4. Do your employees value the rewards superior performance brings? Have you discovered, for example, that money is not everyone's first choice?

5. How often do you bestow rewards? Do you present awards spontaneously, or do people know that there are only specified times when they can hope to gain recognition for their efforts?

CHAPTER 4

A Winning Culture Has Many Cultures

Do you allow microcultures to grow in your company? Do you encourage them or just tolerate them?

Is there a place in your company for talk and meditation? Are your microcultures true to their imperatives?

Do your microcultures work well together? Do they serve the larger purpose of the macroculture? Are any of your microcultures growing out of proportion to their importance?

W hat's wrong with this picture?

A Maybelline executive sits with a group of technicians in a laboratory-like room. Suddenly they encounter a glitch in the computer program they're using to design new packaging for Maybelline products. The executive looks worried. The packaging lab manager reassures her: "Never mind, we'll take all the time we need. At this company, we aim to please, even if it means we're not always on time."

Well, there's nothing wrong with the picture, really. Except that the company is FedEx—the outfit that is absolutely, positively on time. On-time pickups and deliveries, which the company lives by, demand work with the utmost precision. Everything the company does, one might think, would defer to the clock, whether it's opening a new shipping channel, hustling packages through the midnight sort, or even designing a new package for a valued customer.

So what is this packaging lab manager talking about?

He is talking about what I call corporate multiculturalism, which allows for the flowering of microcultures that serve the all-encompassing macroculture.

Let's step back for a moment, and consider the concept of culture itself. Culture—defined by the *American Heritage Dictionary* as "the totality of socially transmitted behavior patterns, arts, beliefs, institutions and all other products of human work and thought"—evolves within all communities and institutions, both consciously and unconsciously. In 1939, the first research on corporate culture was undertaken at Western Electric, a utility. Work groups, the researchers discovered, form cultures which have an enormous impact on how a business functions, and, by extension, on its ultimate success or failure. Every company develops its singular culture, ethos, and specific dictates, and many strive to protect the uniqueness of their own cultures.

Time, Inc., for example, blocked a takeover bid by Paramount, arguing that the acquisition would irreparably damage its culture. The presiding judge agreed, stating that the law could recognize any threat to a corporate culture, if the culture was shown to be palpable, distinctive, and advantageous to the conduct of business.

Strong cultures that succeed share certain common traits. A vigorous culture is well-aligned with the business' goals, motivates employees, and provides an empowering structure that lessens the need for bureaucratic checks and measures. FedEx's culture succeeds on all three counts.

"The reason our culture works," says FedEx senior vice president Mary Alice Taylor, a 16-year veteran who oversees U.S. and Canadian operations, "is its connection to our belief in quality and to providing service to the customer. In 1985, I ran logistics and trucking, and even in the warehouses—where agents service internal, not external, customers—the people realize their roles were connected to everyone else's, and that what they do ultimately services our end customers."

Taylor has pointed to the two key elements of FedEx's edge: microcultures that serve the macroculture and microcultures that retain their own characters.

LET YOUR CULTURE BE YOUR GUIDE— MICROCULTURES THAT SERVE THE MACROCULTURE

Time, schedules, and flawless service characterize the dominant macroculture of FedEx. The company delivers packages: intact and on time. Period. Within that macroculture, there are small, independent, functional units with no allegiance to the clock. They promote innovation and creativity.

In my early days working with FedEx, I was surprised that the logistics information-systems managers with whom I worked would often show up late at meetings—even those they themselves had scheduled. Many didn't bother to return phone calls for days. How could it be? How could they behave like me and my colleagues at the university? FedEx is a company so obsessed with time that every second counts. A huge clock in the Memphis SuperHub counts down the minutes as 8,000 employees race to complete the sort: Every person there is completely conscious of the relentless passage of time. That's the FedEx I knew. I didn't get it. What I didn't understand was the different ways that FedEx employees with different responsibilities view time. In the hubs, time is it. Elsewhere employees can make their own decisions about time. It all depends on what they're doing.

FedEx truck drivers, for example, transport goods in the middle of the night, rarely meeting customers. They climb into the driver's seat of their 18-wheelers already imbued with the corporate philosophy.

"People have perceived truckers as concrete cowboys who think, 'Nobody tells me what to do, I'm my own person,'" says senior vice president Tracy Schmidt, who runs FedEx's integrated air and trucking operations. "That's what attracts people to become tractor-trailer drivers. We try to allow people to enjoy that independence, but we make sure they aren't like the average guy driving a rig. We want our drivers to see themselves as a critical part of the FedEx network delivering the customer's future. Not as just driving a rig."

Many truck drivers see themselves as individualists with no interest in relating to organizations. FedEx realized that such people would never really fit in so it tries to raise its own corps of drivers. Many of its drivers learned to be part of the company when they started out in customer service or in the sorting operation. FedEx desires independence, but it has to be disciplined and focused independence.

A strong, succinctly stated macroculture is an essential asset to a company when it expands into overseas markets. Most American companies run into real problems setting up shop abroad. FedEx learned that when, in 1991, it moved into Asia.

"We'd always tried to manage our international business from Memphis," remembers senior vice president Joseph McCarty, who oversaw the Asian operation. "We had been phenomenally unsuccessful running everything from home because the people we hired in the other countries simply did not live, breathe, and understand the American business and cultural issues. The new organization localized decision-making. That wasn't surprising. It was easy for us to adapt our products for those markets. That wasn't surprising either. But what did surprise us was that our employees in Asia did not share our service mentality.

"We have always recognized that our couriers are the people who have the most direct contact with FedEx customers. In Asia, however, people regard delivery personnel as the lowest form of life in the work chain—like sanitation workers."

Human resources consultants back in the United States had set wage scales and job descriptions based on the earnings of Asian messengers. Consequently, FedEx found itself hiring unskilled and untrained workers—people at the lowest pay scale— to fill its courier slots. To an executive sitting in Memphis, this seemed a perfectly acceptable recruiting policy. To a customer in Hong Kong, it meant disaster. A courier dispatched to pick up three boxes, for example, would absolutely refuse to accept any more than three. In the United States, the FedEx courier was committed to 100 percent customer satisfaction. It looked like 100 percent customer satisfaction would be unattainable in Asia.

The company had to act quickly. McCarty referred to the company's roots. In 1975, when the fledgling Federal Express started large-scale hiring of couriers, it ignored the models of other package-delivery companies. To make their deliveries, REA Express, Airborne Express, and United Parcel Service hired employees used to working at the loading dock. FedEx wanted people who would walk in the front door and deal confidently with receptionists, secretaries, and managers. Such a job description didn't exist in 1975, so FedEx wrote it. The result was a cadre of educated, motivated, and well-paid FedEx couriers. They redefined the job.

In 1994, the company reexamined the courier's role. They saw that many couriers—whose social skills had made them valuable contacts with customers—were spending too much time on the loading dock. Their jobs required them—in addition to picking up, delivering, and recording their package loads—to load, unload, and sort packages at the field stations and hubs. The company determined that it would be much more cost-effective to hire part-timers to unload the trucks, sort packages into the appropriate shipping containers, reload, and deliver to the airports or trucking depots. The valuable couriers now had more time to deal with customers. "What we're paying the couriers for is customer focus," says Taylor. "Providing direct contact, they *are* Federal Express."

In Asia, FedEx had no choice but to break the mold once again. "It took us four years," says McCarty, "and a lot of effort. We didn't want to impose American values in Asia, but we felt we had to keep to our core corporate philosophy. We tried to train the Hong Kong couriers to understand that service comes first, and we tried to train them to understand what FedEx means by service."

Today, when Hong Kong couriers arrive at pickups, they courteously accept customer orders and react competently and intelligently to the unexpected. FedEx devoted a lot of time and attention—not to mention money—to hiring and training the couriers who would be assets to the company. The lesson here is simple: The microculture must have its own character, but it must also serve the purpose of the macroculture.

FINDING THE BEST WAY TO DO THE JOB— MICROCULTURES THAT RETAIN THEIR OWN CHARACTER

A truly strong culture, as opposed to an artificially strong culture, supports multiculturalism. The artificially strong culture dominates every aspect of the company, imposing a universal norm of behavior. For example, during the '50s and the '60s, automotive assembly plants focused unwaveringly on car production first, and everything else, including quality, took a distant second place. That attitude not only affected auto sales when high-quality imports breached our markets in the '70s, but it also bred a type of manager who had enormous difficulty changing from a ship-any-thing-but-ship-it-fast philosophy to a let's-get-quality-and-customer-service-in-place-and-then-ship-the-cars approach. Many couldn't make the transition.

The message is, if your macroculture requires Swiss-watch discipline, then, yes, be good at it. But you had better have microcultures devoted to innovation and improvement. Otherwise, somebody is going to come along and build that better mousetrap before you. You need slack time and resources to nurture innovation. That lesson applies to customer satisfaction as well. Some part of your organization must be accountable for keeping customers first and developing the tools and methodologies to do that.

No matter how time-conscious the FedEx macroculture, the company needs functions within the organization that operate independent of time. POWERSHIP, the popular shipping system that lets customers prepare their own labels and track their own shipments, was a creation of the sales division. Had the company put too much time pressure on that group, that effective new technology would never have made it to market. And yet time was the group's motivator: The final product reduced the time needed to process package pickups.

To create multiple cultures, start by empowering your employees. When employees themselves set their job priorities, they invariably improve their performance and productivity. That is a central conviction at FedEx.

In the hubs, the work is routine and procedural. At the other extreme, there are tasks that I call open adaptive: Those jobs involve coping with and adapting to uncertainty and risk, and employees in such positions continually change their routines in response to problems. Jobs of that type demand intellectual and creative energy.

If you scan the entire spectrum of microcultures, you will recognize a continuum: regimented jobs at one end, adaptive jobs at the other, and a progression toward unrigidity between them.

At the regimented end, employees perform as instructed. Innovation is not the priority, but quality circles do interject an element of continuing improvement. At the adaptive end of the spectrum it's common for subordinates to tell their supervisors what they will be doing, then ask for the resources to do it. For every position, the company grants an appropriate level of empowerment: Everyone is focused on achieving the company's mission.

Fred Smith believes in intellectual development. At FedEx, the managerial cadre is strong because Smith has encouraged the company's leaders to think outside the box: Fred himself at one point investigated the use of dirigibles. Sometimes, his affinity for the novel approach borders on the fantastic—dirigibles, for instance. Who would think of such a thing? Well, back in the early 1980s, Fred Smith did.

The most famous dirigible of all time, the German *Hindenberg*, crashed and burned in New Jersey, in 1937. Following that catastrophe, nobody considered using blimps for anything other than hovering billboards. Still, Smith found their transportation capabilities tantalizing. The size of a football field, the Hindenberg could carry 250 tons at speeds approaching 100 miles per hour. The 50-ton capacity of the DC-10s of the 1980s was meager by comparison.

As it happened, Smith discovered that the development cost for launching a new generation of large dirigibles was simply too great. He encountered similarly overwhelming obstacles when he considered using the Concorde for international package delivery.

Another employee recommended that FedEx sell its hush kits—noise reduction kits developed jointly by FedEx and Pratt & Whitney to control noise in FedEx's own jets—to other airlines. In the spring of 1995, FedEx sold 46 hush kits to Delta Airlines' 727 fleet. As a result of an employee's ability to think beyond the confines of his job description, the company transformed an expense into a source of revenue.

FedEx's separate but linked microcultures work surprisingly well together considering how far apart their imperatives sometimes are.

Before I became involved with the logistics group through the Cycle Time Research Center, my experience with FedEx was that of a customer. Couriers, prompt and well-mannered, regularly delivered packages to me at my home and office. I'd toured the SuperHub operation, where the sight of thousands of people converging out of the darkness to correctly sort a million packages amazed me. That's why the casual, though not unprofessional, style of the logistics and information systems groups surprised me.

How does the rest of the company feel about the apparently cavalier attitude of personnel and information towards schedules, the identifying signature of FedEx? Observing that nobody harbored resentment or suspicion was the beginning of my understanding of the FedEx community. The company's macro culture and the microcultures nurture and support one another. The logistics group and the information systems group—both wellsprings of innovation—respond to distinctly different deadlines.

The message of FedEx's success is clear. The company maintains a macroculture that encourages strong, thriving microcultures. "We have a clearly articulated vision and mission," says senior vice president Perkins. "Every employee—120,000 are scattered all over the world—understands our primary job is to satisfy and delight our customers. The ability to customize services exists, and this ability serves some customer who needs a task performed in a different manner."

The unspoken, but common, attitude among employees is that

delivery must be absolutely, positively on time. Everything they do leads to that. Whatever they are working on must contribute to the company's continuing ability to achieve its goals. Some ideas may not pan out, but those that do, contribute to operational excellence, customer intimacy, or innovation. That's the macroculture of FedEx.

Whether it's a computer chip bound for Silicon Valley or a crucial bank document from Michigan for a Massachusetts house closing, a sorter in the SuperHub waves the same scanner across each package's bar code.

Couriers at both ends of every transaction, completely comfortable with the FedEx tracking technologies, knowledgeably explain all the shipping options to customers. The couriers are also on top of weather conditions and equipment problems that might affect package delivery. "They all know we're here for one purpose only—to serve the customer," Perkins asserts.

Here are guidelines to ensure that a company's microcultures perform at high levels while supporting the macroculture:

Define the Company's Mission and Values in Terms Everyone Can Grasp. Does management's conduct consistently mirror that vision? It does if employees can confidently present a coherent explanation of that philosophy. Company newsletters, closed-circuit television, coaching, and training all help.

See That the Macroculture Is Strong Enough to Support Several Distinctive Microcultures. If the dominant macroculture gets production out the back door, is there another counterculture that focuses on quality, customer satisfaction, and innovation? Are employees able to behave in accordance with the imperatives of their microculture? Does, for example, the production manager drown out the marketing manager's message or is the organization strong enough to hear and balance the two viewpoints? The answers to those questions will mirror the strength of the macro-culture and its ability to foster empowerment.

If a Variant Culture Starts to Emerge from the Macrocul-ture, Evaluate Its Usefulness and Consider Supporting It Rather Than Suppressing It. A case in point is FedEx's Logistics, Electronic Commerce and Catalog (LECC). LECC is a value-added reseller of FedEx services that provides marketing, information services, and logistical solutions for customers, including

- **PartsBank:** A turnkey, 24-hour order-entry, customer service, and warehouse service that features the best possible access to the FedEx network.

- **Integrated Repair and Return:** A domestic, door-to-door, fast-cycle (48 hours) repair service, whereby FedEx manages the pickup, repair, and return of defective computers and other electronic products.

- **Emerge:** Coordinated delivery of product components from two or more locations. Often, the company ships component parts directly from the manufacturer to the end customer.

LECC began, naturally enough, as an internal service. Its mandate was to solve logistical problems and improve coordination of the company's increasingly complex systems. FedEx occasionally offered LECC as a free service to accommodate its customers' logistical needs, and gradually it became a full-blown consulting service and profit center.

Understand That as Job Responsibilities and Goals Vary, So Do the Cultures That Each Job Requires. Employees who per-form routine tasks can thrive within well-structured atmospheres that would paralyze employees whose jobs require a flexible,

responsive approach. Each recognizable microculture within an
organization should enjoy the respect and the admiration of every
other microculture. FedEx provides continual training and coaching, supported by appraisal and compensation systems that reinforce those messages.

The company has also instituted mechanisms that allow people
from other parts of the company to interact with its pilots. FedEx
pilots, like its truck drivers, are pretty much loners. Anyone can
take the opportunity to hitch a ride on a FedEx plane, riding in the
so-called jump seat. It's an unmatchable way to learn about the
pilots and their contribution to FedEx.

Speaking of truck drivers, let me mention here that they—unlike
truck drivers employed by other companies—occasionally help load
and unload the trucks. When people first observe that, their reaction
is that it is a poor use of expensive hands. Wouldn't it be more eco-
nomical to hire part-timers to do the loading and unloading? However, the truck drivers' participation in that process brings them
much closer to the people in the hubs.

**Keep the Macrocultural Focus Strong by Starting Employ-
ees at Entry-Level Jobs That Imbue Them with The Company's
Mission.** Many of the company's top managers started their careers
with FedEx in the hubs or customer call centers, where they gained
an appreciation of the company's commitment to time, cost, quality,
and customer service.

**Keep Employees Informed of Company Progress and Set-
backs as Well as Their Own Personal Performance.**

Survey Employee Attitudes Regularly. Such inquiries go a
long way toward spotting problems before they have a chance to
take hold and cripple the organization. Conduct the surveys annu-

ally or—if many attitude problems are apparent—semiannually, and craft them to elicit the true feelings of employees at all levels of the company.

Do Not Attempt to Superimpose One Culture on Another. It may prove fruitless—even dangerous—to the success of the organization and its mission. When FedEx first started operations in Europe it failed to recognize the particular cultures of each of the many countries it was trying to serve.

....

A CHECKLIST FOR MANAGERS

These questions should give you an idea of whether your company is a cohesive whole and whether its parts fit together well.

1. Do you allow microcultures to grow in your company? Describe some of them.

2. Do you encourage microcultures or just tolerate them?

3. Is there a place in your company for talk and meditation?

4. Do all of your employees understand what their coworkers do? Do they spend time doing others' work?

5. Are all microcultures serving the company's larger goals?

6. Are your microcultures true to their own imperatives?

7. Do your employees understand the relationship of the microcultures to the macroculture?

8. Do your microcultures work well together?

9. Are any of your microcultures growing beyond the proper proportion of their importance to the company?

....

CHAPTER 5

An Ounce of Inspiration Is Worth a Pound of Control

....

Does your company have a leadership evaluation process?

Do your top managers have the right stuff to transform the company? Are the people who work for them truly inspired to achieve company objectives? And— the acid test—does your company achieve those objectives year after year?

Do your leaders have specific skills—in addition to their leadership qualities—that earn the respect and allegiance of employees?

Do your leaders assure that everybody shares in the rewards of success?

Have your managers learned to accept and embrace criticism of their performances?

....

Let's face it, most of us Americans get all bent out of shape when we think and talk about leaders and leadership. Most of us, in fact, feel overmanaged and underled—overcontrolled and underinspired. Consequently, there is a big disconnect between those who lead and those who work for them. At FedEx, however, Fred Smith has shown how to resolve that conflict: how to reconnect the disconnected. Promotion-from-within policies, leadership training that emphasizes both skill-based authority and appropriate styles of self-presentation, and an innovative evaluation program are key. The goal of that training is the attainment of transformational leadership.

MAKING A DIFFERENCE— TRANSFORMATIONAL LEADERSHIP

One way to get a grasp on this slippery subject is to think in terms of the paired categories "transactional" and "transformational." In theory, anyone can learn transactional leadership. All you need is the wherewithal to administer one side of the transaction: the pay, privileges, and perks which are offered—and on appropriate occasions augmented, reduced, or withheld—in exchange for the time, skills, energy, and cooperation of the other side of the transaction. In other words, the transactional leader needs to give nothing personal.

The trouble is, the "other side" does need to give something personal. More and more, in these days of relentless competition and change, employees must give greater efforts, improve their skills, contribute more time, and, with the rise of teamwork and diversity, show greater sensitivity to others. All those demands call for specifically personal qualities of willingness, intelligence, sociability, adaptability, and the like. That being the case, there's something terribly out of whack, even unfair, about transactional leadership. If employees are to give personal qualities, why shouldn't their leaders?

Enter transformational leadership. According to FedEx's *Manager's Guide*, "A transformational leader raises subordinates' awareness about issues of consequence, shifts them to higher level needs, influences them to transcend their own self-interests for the good of the group or the company, and inspires them to work harder than they had originally expected they would." In other words, transformational leaders effect superior, job-appropriate, personal changes in their subordinates.

Consider, for example, the report of Mary Alice Taylor, a transformational leader who is senior vice president for the United States and Canada: "It was obvious that we needed to energize ground operations. We were behind competition in yield. Ground operations had been driving costs down, but I thought there was another level we could get down to if only we could focus everybody on a single objective.

"So, coming into the picture—and I was arriving behind another manager who had been very well-liked by the troops—I needed to do something to get everybody's attention. That's where Best Practice Pays comes in. What it did for us was to get 50,000 employees focused on productivity improvement and customer service. These are two of the key elements FedEx is famous for.

"We decided to take operations to the next peak. Well, here's what happened. We made the next peak, nearer to 100 percent performance than we ever dreamed possible, and our costs grounded out at their lowest level ever. This runs counter to what the so-called experts say. They claim that the closer you get to 100 percent performance the costlier it becomes to squeeze out that extra percent and hold it at that level. What we found was that closing in on 100 percent customer service meant that we had less rework in the process. We didn't have to make multiple trips to customers to correct the problems.

"We made a lot of changes. One involved our courier routes. What was happening before was that, say, two couriers would go out, one with a moderately light load and one with a moderately heavy load. Well, the latter left the station knowing that he would probably not make all of his deliveries on time. If the first courier had worked with the second courier to balance both loads, then both couriers would have delivered on time, and there would have been no slack time in the schedule. What we did was to start Best Practice Pays to get everybody to work more closely together. It gave us that needed extra peer interaction where everybody bene- fited—the couriers, the customers, the company."

The moral of Taylor's story is clear. Let's say, for purposes of illustration, that you work for me and that I am evaluating your per- formance. You might be working at a level adequate to hold your job. Or you might be working, as we say of machines, "at capacity." Or you might even be working at a level higher than even you believed you could: namely, a level above your capabilities. The 1995 film, *Apollo 13*, illustrated how people do reach that third level: You may recall that the NASA contractors and engineers were all discouraged and feared they would not find a solution to a problem that threat- ened the astronauts' safe return to earth. Gene Krantz, mission director, then stepped up and announced to them, "Gentlemen, fail- ure is not an option." His statement energized them: Their spirits ral- lied, and they got the job done. When failure was an "unacceptable option," NASA's engineers did exceed what even they had thought were their limitations. It's by helping you to reach the third level of performance and realize it again and again, for years on end, that my own personal leadership capacities come into play. At that level, nobody could confuse either my performance or yours with average work. But at that level, too, others begin to judge both of us: not just in terms of the fulfillment of a transaction, but as very human beings capable of transforming, and of being transformed.

You can spot transformational leaders only by talking with their subordinates. They will tell you about their accomplishments during the most recent quarter, say, as if they themselves can't quite believe the stories. As for their leaders, they probably can't quite believe it, either. There is something ultimately inexplicable about transformational leadership. That's why, as the *Manager's Guide* says, writers on leadership tend to discuss "popularity, power, showmanship, or wisdom in long-range planning," anything but the mysteries of the thing itself.

FedEx has sketched distinctive characteristics of transformational leaders. These are as follows:

Skills Achievement. One reason that certain corporations have found it relatively easy to cut their employment is that a large proportion of the unlucky are middle managers. Middle managers bring no readily definable skills to the office. The so-called downsizing corporations aren't playing quite fair. Today's indeterminately skilled middle manager is, after all, yesterday's big deal: a generalist. Nevertheless, the contemporary workplace cannot afford people without specific, identifiably hard skills—even those people who are destined by inclination, ambition, or good fortune to be leaders.

In a company that tries hard always to promote from within, leaders rise with their skills. Remember the Peter Principle? That theory held that high performance at one level of skill or responsibility was no guarantee of high performance at the next level. On the contrary, sooner or later, everyone finds himself above his level of competency. It's my observation that FedEx doesn't believe in the Peter Principle. Or, what amounts to the same thing, FedEx runs the risk of flouting the Peter Principle. It must. First, at FedEx, as at every company that promotes from within, the skill with which you do your job is the way to spark notice, praise, reward, and promotion. And FedEx recognizes that in the era of personal leadership, as sketched above, there is no better way for leaders to earn at least the initial respect of their subordinates than by earning a reputation for great skill in their previous jobs.

Maximize Personal Attributes. Employees who are comfortable with numbers and analytical tools but lack social skills or the ability to work as a member of a team are unlikely management material. Leaders must have those skills and ability, and they must take pleasure in working through others: delegating responsibility and measuring and judging performances, and so on. Those characteristics are not as common as you might think. Many people much prefer to work alone, to, as they say, "do it themselves." Many others hate to judge others nearly as much as they hate being judged. FedEx's leadership program keeps watch for people who demonstrate that they aren't effective leaders, and it screens them out early in the process.

Other people, though they like to think of themselves as useful, recoil from the slightest suggestion that they are being used. Leaders know this, and they know how to deal with it. For them, coworkers are both ends in themselves (not used) and means to an end (useful and used). It's not easy to have both those aims in mind simultaneously, but effective leaders are the people who do. Their secret, often, is their personal passion for getting the job done, and they can communicate that passion to others. It's that ability that makes them transformational leaders.

Leaders Must Be Loyal to Their Employees. As Robert Greenleaf, author of *The Servant as Leader,* says, "A new moral principle is emerging which holds that the only authority deserving [an employee's] allegiance is that which is freely and knowingly granted by the led to the leader in response to, and in proportion to, the clearly evident servant stature of the leader. Those who choose to follow this principle will not casually accept the authority of existing institutions. Rather, they will freely respond only to individuals who are chosen as leaders because they are proven and trusted as servants. To the extent that this principle prevails in the future, the only truly viable institutions will be those that are predominantly servant-led."

There's a bit too much Uriah Heep in that formulation. Still, no one can doubt that leadership today is not only a feature that a leader has, it is also and primarily something that a followership gives. "And they don't give it for nothing." Followers expect returns from their leaders. Above all else, perhaps, they want loyalty. They want to be confident that their leader will stand up for them, look after their interests, and tell them the truth.

Leadership Must Seek Partnership Rather Than Impose Patriarchy. Under the old model, the boss took care of the employees. He—and it most often was a man—told you what to do, how to do it, and when he wanted you to do it. And you could be pretty confident that as long as you followed his orders, he would guarantee your job. The new model, however, sees employment as a partnership. Performance is not a question of who happens to be right: What counts is being right. As the intellectual content of jobs rises, subordinates gain a greater share in deciding real and important matters.

Leaders Must Be Bearers of Change. Unquestionably, the most emotionally charged issue in the workplace today is change. Change comes in a full range of guises: improving technology, staffing and restaffing, forming and disbanding teams, shifting markets, retooling for new products, and more. But the most unsettling changes are, of course, downsizing and outsourcing of jobs.

Leaders are, in every sense, bearers of those changes. They must bear up under them, like everybody else. But they must also bear the weight of carrying that news, and they must manage them. Bearing change demands great emotional balance. It demands courage, intelligence, patience, urgency, sympathy, firmness, focus on goals, and care for the human means to achieving those goals. None of this is easy.

Good Leaders Have a Well-Honed Sense of Duty. Many of today's adults grew up in a moral culture that, to say the least, no longer prizes duty. To be more precise, the culture no longer prizes duty to anyone or anything but oneself. People who internalized that culture will not be leaders at FedEx. FedEx asks of every employee, but of its leaders most of all, that they put the interests of the customers, the company, and its employees over and above their own interests. That's where duty calls at FedEx.

I've heard that Jack Welch of General Electric used to say that the problem at too many organizations was that the employees perceive the boss as their primary customer. If, he'd continue, you think of an organization as a pyramid, and everyone is looking inside and up to the boss, the customers see nothing but the employees' rear ends.

Leaders Must Be Able to Take Criticism as Well as Dish It Out. "What's sauce for a goose is sauce for a gander" is not a bit of folk wisdom you would have heard in the old, impersonal, command-and-control workplace. But with the coming of personal leadership in business, the old adage has found new forms. FedEx leaders have responsibility for judging the performance of their subordinates, and subordinates have a responsibility to judge leaders on their performance. The annual Survey-Feedback-Action (SFA) questionnaire is the main instrument of those judgments, and reading them can be pretty painful. As we saw in Chapter 1 Steve Nielsen, who is actually now director of the company's Leadership Institute, found his employees' assessment challenged his assumptions about being boss.

But ladling out the "sauce" doesn't stop with the questionnaire. Its very existence encourages a degree of mutual candor in FedEx offices and shop floors that would have been unthinkable anywhere else 15 or 20 years ago. This might be considered as certain progress in fairness. Note, however, that fairness had little to do with it. The balance of critical responsibility has the effect of keeping both sides on their toes—the better to compete in the marketplace.

Leaders Must Be Endlessly Resourceful. A corollary of loyalty to your employees—and of transformative leadership in general—is providing people with the time, the material resources, and the authority to do a superior job. There is no act of leadership more cruel—or stupid—than assigning a task without simultaneously assigning the wherewithal to accomplish that task.

How often, for example, have you prepared a budget for the following year only to have your boss load your agenda with additional tasks at the same time he slashes your budget by 10 percent? Perhaps you've never suffered such misfortune, but certainly you know people who struggle under such burdens. It usually doesn't happen at FedEx.

Leaders Must Have the "Right Stuff." We spend at least one-third of our adult days on the job. If your manager can't do his job well, how much misery does that add to your already burdened existence? If your manager can't inspire you to greater accomplishments, if she can't excite you about her vision, if she can't convince you of the importance of your work, how likely are you to discharge your duties at a consistently high level? Poor direction is a destructive encumbrance. Neither you nor your company can afford the luxury of bad management.

FedEx's experience can help you turn your managers into leaders who inspire and enhance the experience of your employees:

Transformational Leadership Starts at the Top. Of course it doesn't have to: Well-run companies can foster transformational leadership even if the top person is an automaton with vital signs. One might argue that top-dog transformational leaders are dangerous: They leave so great a vacuum when they go, it might have been better had they never made their marks.

On the whole, however, it's much better to have a living, breathing human at the head of the enterprise: a person who sets a high standard of transformational leadership. Today's business environment demands no less. Furthermore, personal qualities find resonance with personal qualities, not with job descriptions or the expertise of headhunters. It's not that charisma, and only charisma, can summon charisma in others, or that only aggressiveness can call forth others' aggressiveness. It's not necessary that there be a one-to-one match between the personal qualities a leader wants to encourage in her employees and those she possesses herself. But what the top transformational leader does need are real, describable, recognizable, and distinctly personal qualities.

I don't want to say that he or she must have personality, or, still less, be one. That word is now, perhaps unfortunately, synonymous with a funny, eccentric life-of-the-party caricature. But in order for aggressiveness to summon resourcefulness, for example, or for courage to summon imagination, the leader must not only have those qualities, he or she must also be able to project them.

Here's a Warning. A real danger of transformational leadership at the top is that it will generate such heady legends, such glorious headlines, that the lucky executive will come to believe that he and his fabulous reputation are one and the same. Such leaders' heads swell, they act godlike, and they can tolerate no criticism. Sycophantic lieutenants satisfy their every whim. That behavior, if unrestrained long enough, leads to corporate death.

Good long-term leaders, proud as they may be of the work they're doing, never forget that they work with others, and they remain humble before their good fortune.

Let me tell you a story about such a leader. Every year, FedEx invites its executives and customers to the Orange Bowl in Miami, and part of that program is an executive education session. FedEx had set up its Orange Bowl headquarters at the Doral Hotel. I was there to deliver the keynote address, but I was also trying to recruit Mark Gillenson, a University of Miami professor, to join our program at the University of Memphis.

Because I was really eager to hire Mark, I had not only invited him to attend the conference, I also introduced him, from the dais, to the several hundred assembled FedEx employees and customers. The audience acknowledged his introduction with a polite round of applause. Sometime after the program, as Mark and I strolled through the crowd, we saw Fred Smith, said hello, and continued on our way. Smith must have suddenly recognized Mark, because the next thing we knew, he'd chased us down and was telling him about FedEx, the university, Memphis, and what we were trying to accomplish with our cycle time project. He added that he would love to have Mark join our team. After that, there was no holding Mark back from accepting our offer.

CEOs Have Tremendous Demands on Their Time. They must deal with the full panoply of company problems as well as the diversity of personalities in their executive ranks. Institutions of all sorts want a piece of their time for speeches, seminars, and symposia. Effective CEOs learn to master their schedules. Fred's top priority is running the company and doing what he can to help the employees who serve FedEx's customers. He invokes his icon status not to promote himself: Rather, he promotes FedEx, its employees, and their service. For a transformational leader, those are the right priorities.

....

A CHECKLIST FOR MANAGERS

1. Does your company have a leadership evaluation process? Do you expect all supervisors and managers to meet certain minimum requirements?

2. Do your top managers have the right stuff to transform the company? Are the people who work for them truly inspired to achieve company objectives? And—the acid test—does your company achieve those objectives year after year?

3. Do your leaders have specific skills—in addition to their leadership qualities—that earn the respect and allegiance of employees?

4. Do your new managers receive the necessary training and development continually to improve their managerial effectiveness? Does your company recognize that leadership development is a continuing process? Do you have a mechanism for screening out people who lack leadership potential? Are people, in fact, screened out? (At FedEx, it's up to 10 percent.)

5. Do your managers always have—and provide—the tools they need to get jobs done?

6. Do your leaders assure that everybody shares in the rewards of success?

7. Are your leaders faithful to their employees?

8. Are your leaders capable bearers of change? Can you recall a few significant changes brought about by leadership?

9. Have your managers learned to accept and embrace criticism of their performances? Can you recall an employee criticizing your own performance? How long ago was that?

10. Have you developed a series of instruments like FedEx's Survey Feedbacks Action along with periodic surveys of customers?

11. Do your managers consciously make decisions that are clearly designed to benefit the company, customers, and employees? Can you cite a few?

CHAPTER 6

The First Rule Is Change the Rules

Do you and your executives understand today's rules and regulations well enough to spearhead change?

Are the changes you'd like to bring about motivated by the knowledge that your customers will benefit?

Are the people in your organization committed to supporting a political fight for a needed change?

Does your company have mechanisms for enlisting the support of your employees, your customers, your suppliers, the business community, and the general public?

Back in 1971, when Fred Smith was launching Federal Express Corporation, a couple of years before the business began actual operations, he approached the Civil Aeronautics Board to register his airline as an air taxi. He needed the air taxi license in order to fly across the United States without restriction due to a very extensive economic regulatory regime contained in the Federal Aviation Act of 1958.

That regulatory regime, which had been initially enacted the Civil Aeronautics Act of 1938 was established by the Civil Aeronautics Board (CAB). CAB was the principal regulatory agency with jurisdiction over all interstate air carriers, and established regulatory requirements that were intended to promote and protect the nation's developing airline industry. Among other things, the economic regulatory structure in force in 1972 provided for strict controls on entry and competition (through the certification process) and for regulatory oversight and control of carrier pricing, mergers, inter-carrier agreements, and route network expansions. Moreover, the federal economic regulatory structure was primarily designed to fit the requirements of passenger services, not all-cargo services.

Smith faced the obstacle of the 1938 regulation Part 298 which stipulated that a fully-loaded air taxi could not exceed 12,500 pounds—a reasonable restriction given most of the aircraft then in service. But Smith's Falcon jets, which he and his entrepreneurial associates had struggled so hard to select, weighed slightly more than 15,000 pounds empty. They figured that a full load would take the total weight to 25,000 pounds, way over the mandated limit.

From the standpoint of Federal Express' planned operations, the requirement that every carrier must obtain a Certificate of Public Convenience and Necessity from CAB was the most crucial regulatory hurdle. That certification requirement would have effectively prevented Federal Express from getting into business, because the established carriers would have opposed the application and, at the very least, could have delayed Federal Express long enough to kill off its financing. Even if Federal Express could have gotten an initial certificate, it would not have been able to add new cities to that certificate without going back to the CAB (and the same industry opposition) which would have prevented Federal Express from expanding as fast as the demands of its business plan required.

What to do? Smith feared that, unless he found a way either to change the CAB's outdated regulation or to work around it, his fledgling business would abort before he launched a single plane. He and his partners determined that their 15,000-pound Dassault DA-20 Falcons would have to carry payloads of over 6,000 pounds just to pass the financial break-even point.

Back when Smith was dealing with that predicament, MCI's William McGowan faced a similar problem. That entrepreneurial giant was engaged in a long, relentless campaign to change rules that interfered with his game: Those rules gave AT&T a monopoly of U.S. telecommunications. McGowan used to joke that his company was a "law firm with an antenna on top." Smith might have said that FedEx at the time was a control tower with lawyers on top.

In 1971, the CAB finally agreed to hold hearings on Part 298 early the next year. Smith took heart, but he realized he needed to press hard—and not just at the regulatory agency. Smith hired a Washington attorney, Nathaniel P. Breed, who was highly enthusiastic about FedEx's objectives and quite confident of FedEx's ability to overcome anticompetitive opposition by the established airline industry.

On July 18, 1972, the CAB lifted the restriction, allowing air taxis to carry 30 passengers and a 7,500-pound payload. It was a great victory for Smith and his new company. Less than a year later, the company was in business. And though the amended Part 298 Regulation was challenged by ALPA and several local service air carriers in Court, it was sustained on judicial review in December 1973.

The amended Part 298 aircraft size limitation enabled Federal Express to acquire a fleet of 32 Dassault DA-20 Falcon jet aircraft, which had a maximum payload capacity of 6,400 pounds and to commence operations without having to obtain a Certificate of Public Convenience and Necessity from CAB, and without having to confront regulatory opposition from the established airline industry trying to crush a new competitor in the cradle. Federal Express commenced its initial flight operations in March 1973. Under the freedom from certification provided by Part 298, Federal Express rapidly expanded its initial operations to approximately 25 cities across the United States within its first year of operation.

Prior to the CAB ruling, there was *no* overnight cargo transportation business. Eight months later, on March 12, 1973, FedEx flew its inaugural route. Fred Smith had given life to a new industry, one that would create value where none had existed before.

Zillions of references to the contrary, business is not a sport. Business is business. But changing the rules of business—like changing the rules in sports—is so difficult, so expensive, so intensely frustrating that many businesspeople conclude that they would be crazy even to try it. Not Fred Smith.

At FedEx, the first rule is to change the rules. Let's look at what's behind the company's ability to rewrite the rules that stand in its way: first, a willingness to change the game for all the players; and, second, an open playbook.

RESURFACING THE PLAYING FIELD— A WILLINGNESS TO CHANGE THE GAME FOR ALL THE PLAYERS

In the history of business, the players who get to write the rules don't always have customers' interests in mind. Henry Ford, for example, didn't have his customers' interests at heart when he informed them that they could have any color car as long as it was black. But when businesspeople do write the rules with their customers' interests in mind, they gain a strong competitive advantage. That's how AT&T retained its monopoly of the long-distance telephone market for so long: It made sure to provide low-cost, consistently high-quality service to customers. It held that advantage until MCI and then Sprint came along and proved that it could provide the same long-distance service at a lower cost.

By mid-1975, the public demand for Federal Express' service had grown dramatically, and was out-stripping the capacity constraint of Federal Express' Falcon aircraft. It was frequently necessary for Federal Express to operate two Falcons "wingtip-to-wingtip" between Memphis and Los Angeles, and in other dense traffic lanes, to accommodate the surging demand. That stop-gap "solution" was highly inefficient economically, and was stretching the limits of Federal Express' 32-Falcon fleet.

In those circumstances, Federal Express had to obtain authority from the CAB to operate larger aircraft than those permitted under Part 298, in order to accommodate existing and projected near-term traffic demand as quickly as possible.

In September 1975, Federal Express filed an application at the CAB for the grant of a specific exemption to authorize Federal Express to acquire and operate five used DC-9-15 aircraft with a cargo payload capacity of 15,000 pounds. This request was based on the indisputable and fast-growing public demand for Federal Express' overnight door-to-door express service, which was not offered by any other air carrier. Virtually every major U.S. carrier filed in opposition to Federal Express' DC-9 application.

In November 1975, the CAB issued an order denying Federal Express' application "with great reluctance," based on a determination that the authority requested by Federal Express could only be granted through the formal certification process under the regulatory regime established by Congress to govern air transportation services. The CAB ruled that the relief requested by Federal Express was clearly justified by the very strong public demand for Federal Express' unique high-quality specialized express service, but the CAB concluded that it simply did not have the statutory authority to grant that relief through its "limited" power to grant exemptions. The CAB encouraged Federal Express to apply for a Certificate of Public Convenience and Necessity and strongly indicated that it would deal as favorably as possible with such an application.

At that point, recognizing the intolerable burdens that the certification process and the existing aviation economic regulatory structure would place on Federal Express' efficiency, operating flexibility, pricing freedom, and growth potential, Fred Smith concluded that only a change in the basic regulatory scheme, so as to remove air cargo services from that regulatory structure, would enable Federal Express to maintain, expand, and improve the new and specialized air express service it had pioneered.

In the FedEx drama, AT&T's role was played by the major airlines. But history moved a little faster for FedEx than it had for MCI. In January 1976, at the beginning of the new Congressional session, Federal Express shifted its efforts to an all-out effort to persuade Congress to remove the regulatory shackles that were severely impeding the growth and development of Federal Express, and of air cargo service generally. Congress was beginning its long romance with deregulation, and the deregulation target of the moment seemed to be the airline industry. The CAB's denial if Federal Express' DC-9 Exemption Application was "Exhibit A" in that campaign, and the phenomenal growth and exceptional quality if Federal Express' service—and persuasive force of Fred Smith's personality and arguments as Federal Express' founder and prime mover—were the irresistible forces that eventually enabled Federal Express to accomplish the first major revision in aviation regulatory structure since it was established 40 years earlier in 1938.

Federal Express' legislative strategy consisted of a two-phase campaign. First, Federal Express attempted to achieve a minor amendment of the CAB's exemption powers under the Federal Aviation Act to enable the CAB to grant Federal Express (and other new-entrant carriers) authority to operate larger aircraft without going through the formal certification process. The limited initial approach was chosen by Federal Express in the hope that the CAB would support it (which it did), and that the industry would not devote extensive efforts to oppose it so as to enable Federal Express to achieve the fastest possible relief from the increasingly serious capacity and inefficiency problems caused by its continued restriction to the use of the 6,400-pound Falcon aircraft. The second step in the legislative campaign was to seek a more comprehensive revision of the Federal Aviation Act to remove all-cargo operations from most of the existing regulatory controls.

As events unfolded, Federal Express' limited-amendment initiative in 1976 ran into extremely vigorous opposition from two primary sources: (1) Flying Tiger Airlines, which was the dominant existing certificated all-cargo carrier, and saw Federal Express' legislative proposal as both a competitive threat and as a dagger at the heart of Flying Tigers' very valuable existing exclusive licenses, and (2) the Teamsters Union, which detested Federal Express as a non-union company and feared that Federal Express' effort would pave the way toward airline deregulation and the consequent loss of union jobs and economic power in the airline industry. Flying Tigers mounted a particularly vicious attack on FedEx. Robert Prescott, founder and chairman of that freight carrier, testified that Federal Express was invading the "cabbage patch" that Flying Tigers had cultivated. He added, "They are serving off-line points…at a very high price….They now want to trade their motor-cycle in for a Mack truck and get into the air-freight business that we are in." That opposition, and the great political power of orga-nized labor in many key Congressional districts, led to the defeat of Federal Express' limited legislative proposal at the end of 1976.

Immediately following that defeat, at the beginning of the next Congressional session in January 1977, Fred Smith began an all-out effort to achieve the complete removal of all-cargo services from the established regulatory regime. In 1977, although the labor unions continued to vehemently oppose all airline deregulation pro-posals, Fred Smith had persuaded Flying Tigers and the smaller cargo carriers to support the cargo deregulation proposal, which was not actively opposed by the airline industry. In addition, Smith went on a media campaign: He corralled every reporter who would listen, wangled appearances before congressional committees, and so on. He told one reporter: "The government doesn't have to give us a thing—it just has to get out of our way."

Unlike other American businesses that wanted the government to impose protective shields around their markets—the automobile industry was campaigning for protection from international com-petition and Harley-Davidson wanted taxes imposed on large, imported motorcycles—FedEx, according to Fred Smith, wanted only for the government to, "get out of our way."

By midyear both the Senate and the House had introduced bills that would allow FedEx to fly larger aircraft and authorized the CAB to grant exemptions from the regulations when warranted. The commercial airlines attacked the bills, calling them "the Federal Express Relief Bills."

Smith was furiously studying aviation law while the deregulation hearings were underway. J. Tucker Morse, a senior officer of Federal Express holding the position of senior vice president for legal and regulatory affairs at the time, represented Federal Express and told Vance Trimble, author of *Overnight Success*, about the subcommittee meetings:

"We had been sitting in there with the majority counsel of the House aviation subcommittee....We were listening to this young council to House Aviation Subcommittee tell us about how the bill was going to be written and why, or why he didn't want to do this and that. The guy didn't have any idea what he was talking about.

"Fred reached into my briefcase and pulled out the Federal Aviation Act of 1958. He held it in the subcommittee guy's face and said, 'You don't know anything about this act!' Fred took his hands and literally ripped the book in half. And threw it on the table. 'This is what I think of your arguments.'

"And I loved it. I've still got the book; it's a historical document. An effective ploy at the time. Fred is not any giant muscle guy, and this book was probably 250 pages. He just ripped it in half and flipped it on the table. This guy just stopped—bug-eyed. It took strength, absolutely. I still marvel at the thing. It was just extemporaneous. Fred was just so frustrated in Washington, as we all were."

Ploys aside, Smith kept up his public relations campaign aimed at members of Congress, the press, the business community, and FedEx's customers. He drafted FedEx employees to write letters, send telegrams, and telephone their members of Congress. He bombarded his customers with a brochure called "Sometimes Free Enterprise Needs a Little Help." He and several members of his top management team spoke before civic and business organizations across the United States.

It was a highly focused media blitz to help soften legislators. And it might have worked, except for politics as usual. A fight erupted between Representative Glenn Anderson of California and Senator Howard Cannon, chairman of the House's aviation subcommittee. The House passed a version of a bill that addressed air fares for the elderly and disabled. When it arrived in the Senate, Cannon tacked on the "Federal Express Relief Bill" as an amendment. Anderson was enraged; he refused to accept the amended bill even though the Senate had endorsed it with a 73-0 vote. Congress adjourned without passing the bill.

Smith continued to lobby Congress, renting a house in Washington for himself and the small army of FedEx employees and attorneys who were part of that campaign. There were positive signs. Jimmy Carter had just taken office, and he had pledged to tear down the bureaucratic walls that had impeded progress in the transportation industry. Furthermore, the Senate had introduced two bills to deregulate the airline industry, and there were indications that the House would be receptive.

On the negative side, powerful interests headed by Delta, Eastern, American, and TWA promised to fight deregulation to the bitter end. Only one major airline, United, endorsed deregulation. Although Smith expressed concern about the massive interests stacked against him, he remained optimistic that deregulation would eventually pass. He just didn't know when.

Then Smith got a big break. Congressman Anderson, who had torpedoed the so-called Federal Express Relief Bill, changed his tune. He decided to back a bill that would allow all all-cargo carriers, including FedEx, to create an open-entry licensing provision, subject only to fitness review. As subsequently amended and passed, that bill relieved the class of all-cargo carriers from most of the other economic regulatory restrictions relating to geographic scope of service, pricing, and other restrictions. It created for FedEx the eligibility to fly the larger aircraft it needed. Senator Cannon went one better: He amended an unrelated House-passed transportation bill to deregulate air cargo traffic. The bill passed both houses of Congress unopposed. President Carter signed it into law in the fall of 1977. The battle was over, and, once again, Fred Smith had won. The entire air cargo industry had been deregulated. "Hey," Smith shouted when he heard the news, "we're free to fly!"

The amendments went into effect January 1, 1978, and shortly thereafter Federal Express began flying its first few B-727 freighter aircraft, more than two years after the CAB's denial of its DC-9 exemption application. Since that time, Federal Express has expanded its aircraft fleet to include more than 500 aircraft, ranging in size up to 250,000-payload B-747 freighter, and operates air express and air freight services to virtually every country in the world.

Three winners emerged from FedEx's long and costly battle to rewrite the rules. One winner was, of course, FedEx itself. The second was the public, or that part of it interested in fast, reliable delivery service, a.k.a. the customers. The third set of winners comprised the fast, reliable delivery service industry, a.k.a. FedEx's competitors. Why, for heaven's sake, did FedEx have to improve the lot of its competitors?

To answer that we must consider another—perhaps more fundamental—question: When does it make sense to try to change the rules of your industry? The answer to that question is: Only when the changes you seek will benefit your customers, your organization, and (paradoxically) possibly some of your competitors in the industry. Another way I might express that is to say: Never shy away from a change just because it will help others. The greatest changes often do.

Of course, you can't help everyone. Legendary economist Joseph Schumpeter's law of market change as "creative destruction" is not likely to be repealed any time soon. While deregulation of the air cargo business engendered more products, more services, and more promotions—all of which created additional volume for FedEx and its competitors and additional delight for customers— something had to lose. In this case, the loser was the U.S. Postal Service. And there will, no doubt, be others before the fast, reliable delivery business has run its course. But to introduce a major rule change that brings about the demise of some of your competitors is not the same as assuring that all your competition will fail. The latter would be a big mistake.

LET YOUR COMPETITORS FOLLOW YOUR LEAD— AN OPEN PLAYBOOK

Consider another major "rule change" instigated by FedEx that also redounded to the benefit of its competitors. That change required no major political action: It was simply a decision to shake up the price structure. In the mid-'70s, FedEx astonished its competitors by henceforth charging a fixed price for any given service, rather than basing the price on distance, shipping volume, or other variables.

Dave Rebholz, senior vice president, sales and trade services, explained: "The ability to charge a Boise customer the same as a San Francisco customer gained FedEx a lot of new business. That tended to counter the loss of income from charging standard prices. Simplification of the process also lowered our costs." Mike Glenn, senior vice president, marketing, customer service, and corporate communications, explained what the customers got out of it: "A long time ago the way pricing was set in this industry...you could be Digital Equipment Corporation, and if you shipped 500 packages on one day, your rate was X dollars. If the next day you shipped only 100 packages, your rate was completely different because of the courier's and the hub's processing time. To complicate the matter your rate could be influenced by the distance those packages traveled to arrive at their individual destinations. So Digital's people would first have to figure every day how many packages they were shipping, look up the rate depending on volume, then do the same thing for every single package, depending on its destination. The process was time consuming and frustrating. Not to mention the many errors customers made. Then factor in the time the courier needed to take to verify if the customer was figuring the correct rate, and you have some idea of how complicated and time-consuming the process was."

Research showed that customers were confused and frustrated by the pricing structure. "They had nowhere to turn," said Glenn, "since the whole industry priced the same way. So we told ourselves, 'We need to take a different approach to this.' We analyzed the entire pricing structure, this time with the object of making it simpler to use and understand. We discovered that if we would apply a flat rate, 80 percent of our customers would get lower, easier-to-understand rates, while 20 percent would have rates either the same or slightly higher...When we switched over, our customers loved it. The new pricing made their lives ever so much easier."

Added Rebholz: "It revolutionized how the industry priced its services. Once we started it, everybody had to change. And I daresay that it helped all of our competitors and their customers, too."

For some companies the phrase "it helped all of our competitors" would be anathema. Not FedEx. For supremely confident FedEx "helping our competitors" is a sign that a change is worth making.

Let's look at the prescription for any company to change the playing field. What lessons can your company take away from FedEx's experience?

Lesson 1. If you are a market leader and the burden of government regulation is keeping you from expanding your business and serving your customers better, then take the lead and start a campaign to roll back the oppressive legislation. It's never easy. You will find it a daunting process. But, as Fred Smith showed, you can make it happen.

Lesson 2. Let the value of your services to customers, not the value of your changes to competitors, drive the effort for reform. If the change flies with your customers, it doesn't matter whether or not your competitors can copy your change and make it work for them, too. Show that you are the industry leader.

Lesson 3. As you contemplate rule-breaking changes of any sort, remember that if your competition beats you to the punch, and you lose customers because of it, they're not all going to return just because you start offering the same service. For instance, in October 1994, Fidelity Investments introduced annual summary statements that automatically calculated equities purchased, equities sold, net prices, and commission charges. The new statements saved customers a lot of book work. Many other brokerage houses lost customers to Fidelity and, even when they adopted that same service, they were unable to lure those customers back. It's better to be "me first" than "me too."

Lesson 4. If your primary interest in introducing changes is to shaft the competition, you are making those changes for the wrong reason, and they may come back to haunt you. The computer and automobile industries have—time and again—seen such strategies backfire. You might trap yourself in a price war, for example, that would drain the resources of both you and your competitors, forcing you to cut customer services because you can no longer afford them. In that scenario, everybody loses.

Lesson 5. The first step in nongovernmental sorts of change is insightful market research. Before changing its pricing structure, for example, FedEx talked with customers and carefully analyzed their needs. It gathered information, too, from its couriers and customer service representatives. You should always consider detailed market research a prerequisite for making changes. Discover what your customers' stress points are; find out what you are doing that they like. Only then can you decide how to alter your standard operating procedures.

....

A CHECKLIST FOR MANAGERS

Complaints about iniquitous rules standing in the way of progress are hardly rare. If you think that it's time for you to think about revising your industry's rule book, consider these questions:

1. Are there changes you would like to bring about that are motivated by the knowledge that your customers will benefit? Why aren't you making them?

2. Are the people in your organization committed to supporting a political fight for a needed change? Have you made realistic estimates of the cost of such a campaign?

3. Are there executives in your company who can comfortably and effectively make your company's case before regulatory and legislative agencies?

4. Does your company have mechanisms for enlisting the support of your employees, your customers, your suppliers, the business community, and the general public? Have they ever done so?

5. Do you and your executives understand today's rules and regulations well enough to spearhead change?

6. Does honest market research that indicates potentially widespread benefits form the foundation for the changes you propose?

....

CHAPTER 7

Problems Have Silver Linings, Too

Have you made it clear to everyone in your organization that you truly believe that a problem found is an opportunity discovered?

Can you describe innovations that arose from problems: your own company's problems and your customers' problems?

Do your customers naturally think of you as a provider of solutions?

Quick. Summarize—in two words—the driving force beyond the world's economic activity. If your answer is "I want," as in "I want clothes that don't require ironing" or "I want fast, overnight delivery," you're right. A second force—a single word—runs a very close second: "Help," as in *"Help!"* This chapter is about how FedEx responds to diverse cries for help: Some are loud, and others are just barely audible. But here is the remarkable result of FedEx's responses to those cries: it invariably helps itself, too.

When customers—current and potential—face problems they can't solve on their own, other businesses should recognize those challenges as opportunities for them to step in and become indispensable. That's how consulting firms grow and flourish. It's also, in part, how FedEx has grown and flourished.

In a sense, FedEx's mammoth, highly automated Memphis SuperHub owes its very existence to a chorus of corporate cries for help. That "absolutely, positively..." promise—as Fred Smith knew right from the start—is not so easily kept. Keep it FedEx has, of course, but simply keeping promises doesn't keep customers grateful for long. Their gratitude has a way of turning into more demands. The slightest shortfall provokes loud complaints, followed by persistent demands for help. Even the most successful businesses—if they're smart—pay attention and respond to their customers' constant prodding always to improve their products and services.

Hence the Memphis SuperHub. Michael Fitzgerald, a veteran of UPS, whom Smith lured to FedEx, established the SuperHub, which moved the company a quantum leap beyond its former facility: a labor-intensive, straight over-the-ground conveyor hub with multiple belts and slides. The new installation uses state-of-the-art barcode technology to move packages over a complex web of conveyor belts.

The results of those innovations were just what everyone had hoped for: The yelps for help faded. And the new facility did more than solve customer problems. It raised customer expectations higher and forced FedEx to stretch even farther.

So it goes. And so it should and can go for your company, too: customer problems transformed into business opportunities, business opportunities into customer satisfactions, customer satisfactions into higher customer expectations, higher customer expectations into more customer problems—round and round, a virtual circle.

How does FedEx get this circle rolling? FedEx finds opportunities in its customers' problems. It also finds opportunities in its own problems.

BE ALL THINGS TO ALL PEOPLE— FINDING OPPORTUNITIES IN YOUR CUSTOMERS' PROBLEMS

An intriguing question: Where does FedEx fit in the three-part schema devised by my friends Michael Treacy and Fred Wiersema in their best-seller, *The Discipline of Market Leaders*? A dialogue on the question might go like this:

It's a service company, so it should be cultivating customer intimacy, right?

Right.

But it's a service company relentlessly ruled by the clock, so shouldn't it also be dedicated to operational excellence?

True.

But isn't it also true that FedEx is in a highly competitive industry, with insatiably demanding customers? Surely this means that it ought to be devoted to product innovation?

Yup.

I don't mean to single out Treacy and Wiersema. For all business theoreticians, consultants, teachers, and students, FedEx is a confounding company. It won't stay put in anyone's categories. Consider, for example, the story of FedEx and one of its steady customers, Indianapolis-based Boehringer Mannheim Corporation, biochemical division, a large manufacturer of pharmaceuticals and biochemical products. Starting with Boehringer's problem, FedEx took just about every role a company can play vis-à-vis its customers.

Boehringer was suffering an unacceptably high product-return rate from its customers. Its products, expensive biochemicals, are worth millions of dollars. The company might ship a package, via FedEx, only to have the customer refuse to accept the delivery. Wrong address. By the time the product made it to the correct address, it was spoiled. Help!

Time for customer intimacy. Cliff Tillman, FedEx's global sales manager, recalls how FedEx worked with Boehringer to find solutions. "We had some of our operations managers work with the company to drive to the root causes of the problem. Using a business process reengineering technique called process mapping, they traced the flow of the product from the time it was packed in Boehringer's factories, tracking it through courier pickup, air shipment, hub sort, and courier delivery. They also plotted the paper flow among Boehringer, FedEx, and Boehringer's customers, and how Boehringer, its customers, and FedEx communicated with one another when problems developed.

"After they completed the analysis, the team located the many areas causing the mistakes. Boehringer's team members and FedEx's team members worked together and remapped the process, adding various safeguards to prevent the problems from recurring. Changes were then implemented. The new system saved Boehringer millions of dollars, not to mention protecting it from the embarrassment of shipping late or spoiled products to its customers."

Enter now operational excellence. "FedEx benefited from the improvements also," Tillman acknowledges. But the point is not so much that FedEx benefited but how it benefited. Sure, the new process dramatically reduced the number of claims Boehringer filed. And, yes, FedEx could now count yet another appreciative customer. But most important to FedEx is that it emerged from intimate immersion in Boehringer's problems armed with new insights into its own systems and processes, insights it could use in its commitment to attain the highest possible functioning of all its operations.

The general approach to problems at FedEx is, "Show me your problem, and we'll work to find the solution. We don't just ship packages." This viewpoint is a crucial element in the imaginative and innovative shaping of effective, customer-pleasing solutions.

In our Center for Cycle Time Research at the University of Memphis, we worked with an upscale shoe manufacturer to solve a persistent inventory problem. That company manufactures high-end shoes in its U.S. plant and imports certain styles from Europe.

Standard inventory policy for retailers licensed to sell their shoes had been to carry shoes in all possible sizes. For instance, the company manufactured hundreds of 13½ D shoes to assure that each of its dealers carried the size. In many cases, those 13½ Ds collected dust for years on dealers' shelves. Inventory turns were low and cash flow was lower than it could have been had the dealers, who average sales of about nine pairs a day, carried only fast-moving shoe styles and sizes. We determined that if we could focus on those styles and shoe sizes that consumers most frequently purchased, then the company would be able to reduce its inventory carrying costs while providing its dealers with a better—faster-selling—mix of shoes.

We developed economic models to derive our final recommendations. We identified optimal quantities for the shoe styles and sizes that the company should manufacture and the dealers should stock. As for other, less popular, shoe styles and sizes, we recommended that the manufacturer maintain its own inventories. The retailers could simply order those pairs as they were needed, and the company would overnight the merchandise by FedEx.

Had FedEx simply told the shoe manufacturer, "Hey, let us know when you need to ship packages overnight," without designing a complete manufacturing-and-inventory strategy, their sales to hard-to-fit customers might have suffered. However, because we examined the customer's problem in depth, FedEx was able to increase its overnight shipment business, provide useful research from The Center for Cycle Time Research, and generate positive customer feelings.

Okay, you will say, but what about product innovation? It's another critical aspect of the FedEx approach to problems, and FedEx plays it for all it's worth. Consider the opportunity it found in the worldwide retailer of women's clothing and home furnishings' problem. That worldwide retailer of women's clothing and home furnishings had been struggling to get a handle on warehousing and distribution that were in such disarray, it was incapable of even verifying what was and what was not in stock.

On March 23, 1994, the London-based *Financial Times* carried a short item on FedEx's rescue of the retailer. The company, the *Times* reported, "has signed a 10-year contract with Federal Express entrusting its worldwide distribution arrangements to the U.S. logistics company.

"The [logistics] arm of Federal Express will assume joint responsibility for [the company's] supply chain, helping to ensure the most efficient delivery of goods from the retailer's international network of suppliers to its 500 stores in 28 countries.

"Federal Express will also work on developing a global home delivery service by September 1993, enabling [the retailer] to deliver goods direct to shoppers within 24 to 48 hours...

The retailer's new CEO "...predicted the move would greatly improve the company's operating efficiencies...Additional benefits would result from working capital improvements and the ability to respond more quickly and flexibly to customers' requirements..."

The company's critical issues did not magically call FedEx Logistics, Electronic Commerce and Catalog into being. The LECC had been around for some time—since 1987—providing warehousing, transportation, and supporting information services for FedEx's worldwide customers. One LECC manager described the service as "the boutique, the custom shop: We're the people who do it your way..."

Its origins, however, lay in circumstances very much like those afflicting the company—that is, a need for help.

By the time the retailer found itself in trouble, LECC had earned a reputation for delivering effective logistics services—transportation, warehousing, and supporting information systems—wherever it could be of help. Indeed, as the CEO acknowledged, the LECC was more than reputable. It was a real innovation: He had picked it for disaster relief because "nobody else has the systems capability and service culture that FedEx has." Maybe that's why that innovation—born of FedEx's eagerness to see opportunity in other businesses' problems—was, by the time of the retailer alliance, racking up sales that amounted to about 5 percent of FedEx's total revenues.

Could it be that innovations made in response to "I want" problems are riskier than those made in response to cries for help? The story of ZapMail makes you wonder, especially about innovations that anticipate wants.

ZapMail was an expensive technological development. That service got off the ground in the early 1980s, following a search for innovative ways to expand FedEx. Facsimile telecommunications, then an emerging technology, was very threatening to FedEx. The idea was that customers would want, not just overnight deliveries, but near-instant delivery of very high-quality copies. FedEx figured it could deliver almost every fax within two hours. The service cycle involved courier pickup, delivery to a nearby FedEx location for transmission via telephone line or satellite to another FedEx location, then courier delivery of the faxed documents to their ultimate destination.

The mistake was, of course, in gauging the willingness of the public to settle for lower-quality copies. When low-priced fax machines appeared on the market, the public responded enthusiastically. Almost overnight, fax machines were in every office and subsequently in many homes.

ZapMail cost the company three years of effort and a pretax loss of $366 million. No chicken feed. Fortunately, the full impact of its misstep struck when FedEx was riding high, and, because it was in such good shape otherwise, it managed to weather that storm quite well.

By the start of 1995 the company ruled the overnight package-delivery business in the United States. Its split-market share was almost double that of its closest rival, UPS. Other competitors—the United States Postal Service and Airborne Freight—followed UPS.

WE DON'T JUST SHIP PACKAGES— FINDING OPPORTUNITY IN YOUR OWN PROBLEMS

Remember the virtual circle we described earlier, which begins, goes around, and begins again with a customer's cry for help?

Well, sometimes the cry you hear may be your own.

After FedEx constructed its SuperHub, overnight service volume accelerated. The management and information systems the company had been using to control operations were starting to show signs of wear. FedEx soon realized that it needed to upgrade those systems or risk the possibility of compromising customer service.

FedEx executives looked outside the company. The computerized reservation systems the airlines had developed impressed them, and they hired Howard Bedford, a reservation systems expert who, in turn, hired a systems team—from such companies as IBM, Avis, and American Airlines. It wasn't long before Bedford had recruited some 150 highly skilled technologists to develop FedEx's automated transaction processing systems.

That group gave birth to COSMOS—Customer Oriented Services and Management Operating System. The first version, which lacked essential tracking features, was relatively crude by today's standards.

Today, the company's master computerized information system links all the company's strategic information systems. COSMOS connects the physical handling of packages with information concerning each shipment—from the time the customer requests service to the package's delivery.

The company greatly improved COSMOS in the early 1980s with its first positive tracking and status information system. It was a dream come true for Fred Smith and FedEx. The ability to track every package in the system enhanced the reliability of the delivery guarantee and provided yet another valuable service for customers.

In fact, with COSMOS, FedEx hit some kind of record in jackpot innovations: By that, I mean innovations that give birth to other innovations. Out of COSMOS, for example, came the following:

- SuperTracker, a computerized tracking system that tells the company and customers where any package or document is at any moment—from pickup through delivery.

- DADS, a digitally assisted dispatch system that communicates to couriers through computers in their vans. DADS provides quick courier response to dispatches and allows them to manage their time and routes efficiently and accurately.

- POWERSHIP, the software for customers' on-premise computers, which now process about one-third of all FedEx shipments. The POWERSHIP systems provide automated billing, allow customers direct access to their package information, and supply detailed information and shipping instructions for international shippers.

- CAGE, a system developed to track both incoming and outgoing shipments held for clearance in U.S. customs sheds. CAGE ensures that all packages comply with regulatory requirements.

- EDR (Electronic Delivery Record), a security system that uses bar code technology to associate each package with a customer's signature.

- CERPS (Customer Exception Request Processing System), a system devoted to processing complaints or requests for exceptions.

It includes POD (proof of delivery records)—the system's most frequent request.

- CSW (Customer Service Workstation), a system that shows all relevant information about any FedEx customer, used extensively by customer service representatives to handle customer orders, inquiries, and complaints.

Here are guidelines that can help you turn your customers' problems into your company's opportunities:

Recognize That Problems Are Inescapable, and Unending. Your strategy should be to stay ever alert for problems to confront and turn into opportunities. The world, particularly the business world, comprises infinite possibilities, any of which can generate the next crisis. All endings are new beginnings. In business there is no rest.

Understand That Many—If Not Most—External Problems Are Really Customers' Cries for Help. The ability of your company to solve their problems is a test of your ability to retain customers.

Companies whose customers never complain or cry "Help!" commonly overlook the opportunities embodied in their customers' problems, and those customers simply take their business elsewhere. To preempt such moves, do market research—especially, and persistently, through your frontline employees, the people in daily contact with customers. Also conduct focus groups. Gather representative samples of customers and ask questions or pose situations that elicit their true feelings about your company's products and services.

If A Customer's Problems Are Mostly In Your Court, Try Not To Solve Them On The Customer's Nickel. You may be tempted to kiss off customers and avoid additional costs: Operations people are particularly likely to take that approach. Naturally. They're the ones who bear first-order accountability for costs, and they're not generally inhibited by any personal relations with customers. Be on guard. Problems really are opportunities, which means that additional costs generally turn out to be investments in problem-solving skills that you can later "sell" elsewhere.

Of Course, There Are Going to Be Some Customer Problems That You'll Be Unable to Solve. Many of those "I wants" and "Helps" will be unreasonable. Use common sense.

Don't Be in the Railroad Business; Be in the Transportation Business. Once you broaden your mandate, you'll discover that you've dramatically increased your ability to reap opportunity from other people's wants and needs.

Don't Stop with Your Customer. Your customer's customer is a source of opportunity, too. FedEx worked with Boehringer Mannheim and its customers to resolve the intractable packaging problem.

Does Your Company Have Low Self-Esteem? Does modesty inhibit your helping other companies out of their difficulty? Don't let it. Your vantage point is unique: It is built upon the accumulated experiences of your company and your employees. And this uniqueness is valuable to others; that's what your customers pay you for.

Always Look at Your Company with an Objective Eye. How often has it generated an innovative solution to tough customer problems? Has your company effectively countered its own internal problems? Have all your company's solutions contributed to the well-being of your customers and your company alike?

....

A CHECKLIST FOR MANAGERS

Does your company turn problems—your customers' and your own—into opportunities? Take this short test to find out.

1. Have you made it clear to everyone in your organization that you truly believe that a problem found is an opportunity discovered?

2. Can you describe innovations that arose from problems: your own company's problems and your customers' problems?

3. Is there a process—known to employees at every level of your company—for acting on problems and getting your company focused on their solution?

4. For, say, the salespeople who are in closest touch with your customers, have you insured open lines of communication to other departments where employees are receptive to their customers' issues?

5. Do your customers naturally think of you as a provider of solutions? How many of your customers regularly turn to your company for help? How often?

6. Do you reward employees for finding new and challenging problems?

7. Do you anticipate your customers' problems, making them aware of difficult situations even before they recognize them themselves?

....

CHAPTER 8

Software Equals Savings, Service, and Sales

How much of your product value comes from information and how much from the product itself?

Are you making the most of the information that your company gathers in the course of its day-to-day business dealings? Have you dissected every operation to be sure?

Have you made significant investments in information systems that are completely up to date, easily accessible, and staffed with exceptional personnel?

Do your information systems allow your customers convenient, direct access to your goods and services?

The world has entered a new age of hypercommunications. And those companies that hope to have a chance to lead their industries and dominate their markets will need to master those new technologies. But there's more to the new world than that. Most companies are under increasing pressure to accomplish more with less: They want to improve service while they cut costs. Many large companies have discovered that they can resolve this apparent paradox by developing innovative software to support their information systems. Because markets and industries—and even businesses within the same markets and industries—need different kinds of information, their managers must continually adjust and upgrade the technologies they deploy to obtain, store, manipulate, and share information. As a consequence, companies almost inadvertently discover that they have new and valuable products on their hands: the information they produce and the technologies they've developed to produce it.

Fred Smith recognized the power of information technology early on. An economic advantage of information technology is that its cost continually decreases while its benefits continue to grow. FedEx has found that its software allows its customers to do more for themselves. As we will see in this chapter, it uses software to make it easier to do business with FedEx; it uses software so that customers would rather do business with FedEx; it uses software that helps its customers do business with their customers. It uses software to cut its own costs. FedEx proves, day after day, that with the right software, the best service is self service.

Once when I was in Smith's office, he said to me, "Years ago, Sam Walton told me, as he sat right where you now sit, 'Everyone thinks Wal-Mart is successful because we've put big stores in small towns—that we simply benefit from economies of scale. The real key to Wal-Mart's success, however, is that we learned to substitute information for inventory.'" Fred Smith quickly absorbed Walton's lesson, and he put it to work for FedEx.

FedEx has pioneered many new markets through the uses of information technology. As Fred Smith told an interviewer in 1994, FedEx had become the logistical arm of a society that is "built around service industries and high-technology endeavors in electronics and optics and medical science." In 1987, to provide warehousing and distribution services for its customers worldwide, for example, the company inaugurated its FedEx Logistics, Electronic Commerce and Catalog (LECC) division.

FedEx itself counts on information technology to boost growth and flatten costs. According to Fred Smith, "We're getting a higher payoff from information systems than from adding aircraft. It lets us save potentially hundreds of millions of dollars." In the hubs, for example, the company has installed bar code scanners that help process packages along the system of conveyors much faster and with fewer errors than the manual methods the company used earlier.

FedEx—ever since its first days—has recognized that good information is key to success. Over the years the company has found new ways to make the most of what it knows. How has FedEx made knowledge pay off? It created information services for customers, information externalities, and transactions that create knowledge and power.

SURFING THE NET WITH FEDEX— INFORMATION SERVICES FOR CUSTOMERS

What is FedEx's single most traveled route? You may have guessed Memphis to Tokyo, or New York to Memphis to Mexico City. But you'd be wrong. Its single busiest route is the information super-highway—the Internet, or the Net.

FedEx, as businesses go, depends heavily on data networks. Almost two-thirds of the company's shipments are made via POWERSHIP, the company's system for order-taking, package-tracking, information-storing, and billing, or via FedExShip electronic shipping systems. FedEx's goal is to have all its customers online by the year 2000.

FedEx is also on the Web. The Internet's World Wide Web has been around for only a few years, but already FedEx has made good use of it. The company, which now moves almost 2.5 million packages daily, introduced its Web site in the fall of 1994. Its home page, the introductory screen to its Web site, gives FedEx customers access to a great deal of useful information, including its COSMOS database. Some 18,000 customers a day click their way through FedEx's Web site, completely on their own. It saves the company money, and FedEx expects to see that increase proportionately as additional customers learn to navigate the Net. *Business Week* cited FedEx as one of America's leading-edge companies: It makes the most of the Web's technology to provide new levels of service to customers.

To help its customers move their businesses online, FedEx provides them with specialized software, FedExShip. FedExShip automates the process of shipping. The days of manually filling out forms and carting packages to a FedEx drop-off box are nearly over.

Using their own computers and FedExShip, customers can schedule pickups, track and confirm deliveries, print bar-code labels, create and maintain a list of package destinations, and track historical information. By helping its customers do business online FedEx, as we saw in chapter 6, is changing the rules to benefit the customer.

In a recent interview with the *Memphis Business Journal* FedEx's manager of electronic commerce marketing, Steven Braun, says, "It's important to realize that FedEx's aggressiveness with new technology comes from a continued desire to meet customer needs...As companies develop new ways of doing business, FedEx will develop new and innovative ways to help the customer meet their changing business needs."

FedEx has also brought the technology home, so to speak. Said Susan Goeldner, FedEx's manager of Internet technology, "We saw the success of the package-tracking site and said, 'Wow, I wonder what we could do on the inside?'" FedEx created its Intranet, the company's private Web site, accessible through the Internet's World Wide Web. The company has established 60 such sites, and every day it adds more. Indeed, FedEx has provided some 30,000 of its worldwide employees with Web-browsing software that helps them access the Web, and it continues to add Web pages for internal company use.

FedEx has devised another tool that quickly proved its value: With IA Corporation, the company introduced the Domestic Customer Invoicing (DCI) System in 1995. It didn't take long for DCI to become the world's largest client/server imaging and work-flow system. It scans, reorganizes, and stores the images of one million airbills daily at a central server, and then it sends those images out to remote data-entry (client) providers. Previously, the company delivered paper airbills overnight to the service providers for data conversion. "The DCI System represents a milestone in

FedEx's migration to client/server computing," said Dennis Jones, FedEx's chief information officer and senior vice president of the information and telecommunications systems division.

FedEx envisions limitless possibilities to the improvements it can realize on the Internet and continues to explore new opportunities for both customers and employees: faster access to information, interactive communications, and reduced response time to customer inquiries of every sort.

USING "EXTRA" INFORMATION TO GENERATE REVENUE— INFORMATION EXTERNALITIES

I travel quite frequently, and I never check my luggage. Never. When I speak at an out-of-town meeting or seminar I need my suits and my slides. That's why I always carry my own bags. To send them in the care of the airline has been, far too often, to send them directly into a nameless abyss.

And that cautiousness raises an intriguing question: Why do I "absolutely, positively" trust FedEx to do on its planes what I never trust other airlines to do on theirs?

For one thing, I can't think of any other airline that has an internal information system to track and assure on-time delivery of baggage. There is no such passenger carrier today. Maybe that will change, sometime.

If the airlines had systems comparable to FedEx's, here's what could happen whenever I was traveling: My wife would be able to sign onto the Internet and learn my exact location, every step of my trip. She would know whether I was in the air and how close I was to my destination. If I happened to be in a cab, she'd know its number and where the cab was taking me. And, with that information, she would be able to phone the taxi and speak with me directly. FedEx technology is already that sophisticated.

Now look at how FedEx uses its information capability to make money—in a matter of speaking—on the side. I call this phenomenon an "info-externality." Externalities, in the lingo of economics, are the enterprise's by-products that don't appear on—that is, they are external to—the account books. Most externalities—like the exhaust that belches from coal-burning energy plants—are quite nasty, but some are nice and useful. Take a familiar example from the media. Among the products of TV networks that never appear on their books are TV program schedules: a sort of information exhaust. Networks used to issue their schedules in ways that profited no one. Until, that is, *TV Guide* came along and learned how to make a lot of money with the networks' information.

Another example: American Airlines developed SABRE, its fabled ticketing and reservation system. In that case the info-externality is a capability—one that far exceeded its own internal needs. So why not "externalize" the capability à la *TV Guide* but, in this instance, retain the revenues for oneself?

Why not, indeed? In the new world of hypercommunications, any manufacturer of information-processing hardware is also, potentially, a producer of marketable information services. Motorola, for example, estimates that almost 80 percent of its product value will soon be software-based. Only the remaining 20 percent is hardware-based. Its biggest initiative right now aims to make Motorola the world's premier software company.

Almost from the start, FedEx recognized the market value of the information services it provided. It was among the first large

American companies to use information technology—its extensive and complex tracking systems—to improve customer service, reduce operating costs, and spin off a revenue-generating capability: its FedEx Logistics, Electronic Commerce and Catalog (LECC). FedEx understood, even back in the early 1970s when most companies had minuscule information technology budgets, that its information-services software was potentially a half-billion dollar business. Indeed, today it is.

FedEx, now a $10-billion company, spends $500 million annually on information technology development plus millions more on capital expenditures. The company has learned, too, that its info-externalities do not necessarily have to be inexpensive or money savers. Before FedEx initiated its Web page, customers who wanted to track their FedEx packages could dial a toll-free telephone number. Once the Web page was up, customers were pleased to go on-line for that information even though it meant paying access fees to Internet service providers or such on-line services as America Online.

Customers have good reason. Not only do they have a certain fascination with the Internet, they also recognize that there's a small degree of technological cachet associated with accessing account information through the World Wide Web. Many customers love the graphics and hypertext links that let them click on highlighted words and phrases to reach additional detailed information about related subjects. Of course, many FedEx customers still take some comfort in the backup toll-free number—and real live customer service—that remains in place.

HARVESTING INFORMATION— TRANSACTIONS THAT CREATE KNOWLEDGE AND POWER

Many companies fail to recognize that information transactions are knowledge generators. And knowledge, as we all know, is power. Let me explain what I mean. Every time I book a hotel reservation, I request a nonsmoking room. From the hotel's perspective, my preference is knowledge. As the hotel accumulates requests like mine, it can make sure that the number of available nonsmoking hotel rooms matches the number of guests who insist on nonsmoking rooms: It has improved its ability to fill the hotel to capacity. Theoretically, though perhaps not practically, the hotel could bring in revenue by selling its nonsmoking-room-only knowledge to other hotels.

This convertibility of information to knowledge to power and revenue is eminently transferable. But your managers and employees must have the acuity to spot the opportunities. People convert information *systems* into applications unimagined by their designers. FedEx's PRISM system—a computerized information system that maintains human resource management programs and employee records—is a case in point. The system handles databases on hiring, transfers, promotions, performance reviews, awards won, employment applications, and other related employee files. According to Jim Perkins, FedEx's human resources chief, "PRISM frees our people so we can maximize productivity. In every station across the world, human resource managers receive all kinds of inquiries. PRISM supplies that information electronically."

But PRISM also illustrates the company's ingenious ability to extend the application of information systems. In the words of Cindy

Walker, senior specialist, personnel systems, "You can log onto PRISM using a terminal or PC anywhere in the company—provided that it is connected to our information system mainframe—to retrieve any authorized information you need. Well, that's great. But what about employees who need that information but are off-site in a hotel room, a restaurant, or at a seminar? They can use outside telephone lines to access PRISM, but it's slow and expensive.

"We decided to speed up the process and contacted a vendor that has developed a special radio device you can connect to your laptop computer. It's along the lines of a cellular phone but more powerful. All you need is the radio device and accompanying software for the laptop. Employees just dial in and log onto the mainframe. It doesn't take long. And there are no telephone lines that you need to hook your computer to.

"Jim Perkins tells about paging one of our managers who was in a taxi in the middle of downtown Chicago. The manager used his cellular phone to return Mr. Perkins' call. Mr. Perkins explained that he needed such-and-such a document. The manager pulled out his laptop, attached a radio device, logged onto the home office's mainframe, and called up PRISM. Within seconds he found the document that Mr. Perkins had requested, and he directed the system to deliver it directly to Mr. Perkins's fax machine. While they continued to talk, the manager told Mr. Perkins, 'I think the document is on your fax machine.' Mr. Perkins walked over to the fax, and sure enough, it was there. All within minutes. And all from one of his managers in a taxi in the middle of Chicago.

"That demonstrates how we keep in touch. You can be a FedEx employee anywhere in the world: We can reach you, or you can reach us. That's how powerful our communications are."

In Jim Perkins' words, "What makes all of this unique is that PRISM frees our human resource people from the paperwork burden normally associated with our function. It makes the administrative part of our jobs a servant to us instead of our being a servant to it.

"Our human resource information systems are benchmarked worldwide. We just returned from an international conference where we received all kinds of flattering comments about PRISM. It was apparent that our system was unique."

Improvements in information systems often come hard. Alfred R. Pozos, former director of the American Productivity and Quality Center's International Benchmarking Clearinghouse in Houston, says, "Many [companies] either grow arrogant, burn out, or encounter internal obstacles that stop them from changing." But there are strategies that companies can consider.

Examine customer problems, and analyze them in detail. Often you will find that you have the information sources that can address their problems. Your information resources may help customers do something of value—something they have not yet recognized. It's up to you to lead the way. Your company should be making extensive investment in interorganizational information systems. Those are systems that connect you to your customer, your customer's customer, your vendor, or your vendor's vendor.

Never Discard or Ignore the Potential of "Information Exhaust." Hotels, for example, discard all kinds of potentially useful—even profitable—information they collect about guests: their eating habits, entertainment preferences, and the like.

When New Businesses Seem to Be Emerging from Such "Information Exhaust," Evaluate Their Potential to Stand as Separate Units That Generate Revenues and Profits. To make successes of those units, you should assign them permanent personnel. FedEx demonstrated the importance of taking those steps when it introduced its logistics services. The seriousness with which it proceeded contributed to its becoming a successful logistics consulting division.

Your Market Research People Should Know What Information Your Customers Find Useful. They should be examining your customers' habits, needs, and expectations in sufficient detail to anticipate ways your information sources can help them.

Integrate Your Information Systems. Structure them in such a way that whenever new information is entered, all related files and databases will automatically be brought up to date. FedEx's customer orders that enter the system through the company's Web page find their way to COSMOS, FedEx's global package-tracking system. Each courier's route planner—an electronic mapping tool—facilitates pickup and delivery of those same customer orders. A product movement planner schedules those orders through the company's global air and courier operations. The customer information finds its way into a customer service representative's computerized information file. The company tracks the shipments through POWERSHIP and FedExShip, customer-based systems for tracking and shipping packages. Such well-integrated systems cost plenty of money and implementation takes lots of time, but it will save you—or make you—money in the long run.

Your Company Should Have a Chief Information Officer. That doesn't mean that in smaller companies someone has to hold that job full time. What it does mean is that you should assign someone that responsibility. That person should have both technical know-how and business sensibility to spot revenue and customer service opportunities. If you already have a chief information officer, does that position change hands frequently?

A real danger of changing chief information officers as frequently as football coaches is that incumbents don't have enough time to get their feet on the ground before they're replaced. Exploring information technology opportunities takes thought, analysis, and direction—none of which is possible when you're playing musical chairs in the information systems office. Although it's not unusual to see turnover rates as high as 50 percent for that position, FedEx, in its entire history, has had only four CIOs.

Dennis Jones, FedEx's chief information officer, describes FedEx's systems area: "The utility of our information technology function really begins with the fact that we have a CEO who clearly understands the value of applying information technology to the business. He understands that to the point that he can provide a conceptual set of specifications. We do not have the issue that you see throughout industry, that the CEO is removed from the information technology aspect of the business. Smith knows that information technology is more than a technical function; it's a function that has a strategic value because the essence of our business is taking a basic service and adding information technology services to transform it into a value-added product. And that's very important. Any company can move freight from point A to point B. But the way you make it a valuable product to your customer is to wrap it with intensive information technology capabilities."

Maintain a Critical Attitude toward Improving the Information Systems Ventures You Now Have in Place. Can you do them better? How can you provide more and better services for your customers with the information systems you have available?

The competition is tough. When FedEx introduced its FedExShip service, UPS announced a similar plan the same day.

FedEx and UPS initiated same-day delivery service literally within hours of one another.

Your Information Systems Should Serve Your Employees or It Will Never Be Useful to Your Customers. FedEx's PRISM system is a perfect illustration. Employees can tap into the system to retrieve personnel documents and information. They can elect to have those records faxed to them. Soon ORION (Optically Recorded Information On-line Network) will support data entry. That technology deploys optical scanners at key locations throughout the company, and employees at remote locations can use high-speed scanning to enter information into PRISM. The new information automatically updates all the linked PRISM databases.

....

A CHECKLIST FOR MANAGERS

Every company that thrives in the coming decades will have learned to leverage its information systems to enhance revenues, improve customer service, and maximize profits. Consider your company in light of your answers to the following questions.

1. How much of your product value comes from information and how much from the product itself?

2. Have you identified services your company could provide that would save your customers time and money?

3. Have you evaluated your company's information systems to find whether your customers might benefit from any embedded capabilities?

4. Are you making the most of the information your company gathers in the course of its day-to-day business dealings? Have you dissected every operation to be sure?

5. Has your company formed divisional spin-offs from its "information exhaust"? Do those separate business units generate revenue and profits? Are the employees dedicated to those units or do the units have to borrow staff from the company's "real" business?

6. Have you made significant investments in information systems that are completely up to date, easily accessible, and staffed with exceptional personnel?

7. What percentage of your research-and-development budget do you allocate to keeping your information technology at state-of-the-art levels?

8. Are all of your management and executive personnel comfortable with today's—and tomorrow's—information technologies?

9. Does your company support a continuous educational effort to keep everyone on top of current and emerging technologies?

CHAPTER 9

He Who Hesitates Is Lost (But, Remember, Look before You Leap)

When everyone else tells you to stop, do you have the courage to stick to your guns?

When you follow a hunch, and it fails, do you approach the problem from another angle, or do you shelve it permanently?

Have you encouraged your financial people to take unconventional approaches when they assess inventive proposals?

A common misconception about business is that management decisions are rigorously analytical. Nothing could be further from the truth. As a general rule, the more highly placed the manager making the decision and the more important its consequences, the more instinctual will be the thinking that goes into it. First-line supervisors may ground their actions on the numbers: labor hours, expenses, quality-control levels, and the like. But at the top of the corporate pyramid, the CEO often acts on a hunch. This chapter is about those hunches, how FedEx uses hunches to conduct its business, and how you can use them in conducting yours.

What about FedEx allows it to make the most of its hunches? Its executives have the courage to act on their experienced-based hunches and allow others in the company that same freedom, and there is company-wide determination to let hunches overrule the financial experts, or "quantoids."

Note that while certain hunches may occasionally turn out wrong, FedEx does not make uneducated guesses. An old story about William MacNeill Whistler, the irascible American artist (who painted—among other subjects—his mother), illustrates the point. He was testifying as an "expert witness" in a case involving the authenticity of another painter's work, when the opposition's lawyer tried to belittle his judgment by pointing to the astronomical sum he was being paid to provide an opinion that required only a few seconds of his time. Whistler, in a fury of indignation, shot back that an entire *lifetime* of experience had gone into his opinion, and that it was right.

Most CEOs could say the same about their hunches, instincts, gut responses, inspirations, whatever you want to call them. They may be shots in the dark, but the hand that holds the revolver is experience.

WHEN YOUR INSTINCTS APPEAR WRONG TO EVERYONE ELSE—THE COURAGE TO ACT ON EXPERIENCE-BASED HUNCHES

Still, every experience-based hunch includes a large element of faith. Not religious faith, but the worldly faith that Walter Kaufmann, the noted translator of Nietzsche's works, wryly defines as an "intense, usually confident, belief that is not based on evidence sufficient to command assent from every reasonable person." Such faith is bound to prompt disagreement—perhaps hot and heavy disagreement—from those reasonable persons we call colleagues.

Such, at any rate, was Fred Smith's faith in FedEx, and in the early days he needed it, badly.

FedEx did not have a good start, to say the least. On the night of March 12, 1973, Smith and his closest associates gathered at a small airfield in Memphis, to await the first planeloads of overnight-delivery packages. Memphis was, even then, the "hub," but the "spokes" that night ran to only 11 cities, all in the South and Southeast, and all within 500 miles.

Workers stood around, too, ready to sort the arriving packages and send them to their final destinations. The FedEx technology consisted of a puny gravity-feed conveyor belt, a temporary sorting table in an old World War II wooden hangar, and a number of taxis and limos hired for the occasion. Some employees were ready to use their own cars to supplement deliveries. It was a scene that made "shoestring operation" sound grandiose.

But the morning and afternoon of March 12 was promising enough. Salespeople and agents had phoned Fred Smith with optimistic forecasts for the first night's run. It looked great, they said. By midnight, virtually everyone connected with the company was at the airfield: Smith, his wife, most of FedEx's corporate officers, the back-office employees, and so on. The atmosphere was Broadway, opening night, waiting for the reviews to arrive. Rather than reviews, however, Smith was awaiting numbers—numbers of packages in the cargo bays of the incoming planes. Henry Meers, now managing director of Merrill Lynch & Co. Inc., was there for the occasion, and remembers the anguish he saw on some of the faces.

Right at midnight the six Falcon jets, their engines screaming, landed and taxied up to the old hangar. The pilots shut down the engines and flung open the cargo doors. The assembled employees peered into the holds.

Empty.

Well, not exactly. The six jets brought six packages to Memphis—one, a birthday present from Fred Smith for an associate.

The worst of it must have been the chorus of I-told-you-so's echoing in Fred Smith's mind. Merely reaching that night and its crushing midnight disappointment would severely test any person's faith. Bankers, investors, industry experts, government regulators—most of the people he had approached for help had told him that the idea of an overnight-delivery service was pure folly. Nobody could pull it off. And now, right there in those empty cargo bays, was the proof. Many who witnessed the March 12 debacle told Smith that he had made a valiant effort, but the ball game was over. Try your hand at something else, they suggested.

But he wouldn't. On the contrary, he and his associates regrouped, still convinced that the business would eventually flourish. They reconstituted themselves as a task force and met behind closed doors for more than two weeks—16 hours every day—to discover what had gone wrong, and why.

They concluded that FedEx had selected the wrong cities for

the service. Two factors should have determined the cities on which FedEx should focus: the numbers and types of a community's businesses and its existing air cargo suppliers. Location was not a determinant, as the entrepreneurs had originally believed.

New Orleans provided a good negative example. For many years, Delta Airlines had served that city well and had established an air-freight business that local companies liked and used. Moreover, New Orleans lacked an extensive manufacturing base with corporations always urgently in need of parts and materials. Rochester, New York, on the other hand, perfectly filled the bill for overnight-delivery services. Its thriving economy supported such growing companies as Kodak and Xerox, but it lacked adequate air cargo support. In the end, the task force identified 26 such cities, and advised FedEx to try again.

The second time it worked. That first evening, on April 17, 1973, FedEx delivered hundreds of packages, and before long, it was handling thousands of packages daily. Today FedEx carries almost 2.5 million packages every night. It was one of the greatest comebacks in business history.

Our focus, however, is on faith, the faith that allowed Fred Smith to persevere despite the skepticism of everyone from the Yale professor who gave him a feeble "C" for the paper in which he first sketched his scheme, through all the journalists, CEOs, investment bankers, insurance executives, and the like who, in the years that followed, consistently gave him that same grade.

In all that time Smith was following his instincts. Indeed, if he had attended to the numbers and followed a more "scientific" course of action, as most of his advisers suggested, he might never have founded an overnight-delivery business. The numbers were all wrong. Had he heeded the numbers or the advisers who relied on them, this book would be about UPS. But his faith, his instincts, his vision—whatever it was—was strong enough to overcome all sorts of bad news, gloomy predictions, and depressingly skeptical advice.

LET A THOUSAND HUNCHES BLOOM— THE COURAGE TO ALLOW OTHERS TO ACT ON THEIR HUNCHES, TOO

It's one thing to have entrepreneurs or CEOs use their instincts to make decisions; it's altogether another thing to have managers throughout the company do the same thing. That's one of the unusual aspects of FedEx. The general rule may be that lower-to-middle levels of an organization make decisions based more on numbers than on instinct, but FedEx is the exception that proves it.

Take next-day afternoon service. Before FedEx introduced that service in 1989, it had a thriving business in overnight delivery. When FedEx first considered offering a discounted price for afternoon delivery, managers had many concerns. Finance and marketing constructed a model that clearly indicated the new service would severely dilute sales levels of the premium-priced overnight delivery. Why, the skittish asked, should FedEx endanger its own market share? They worried that there was just so much business to go around. Why devaluate a portion of that market for a lower-priced service?

But when FedEx managers approached customers, they were able to examine the proposed service more thoroughly. Their perceptive investigation of the market revealed a latent, pent-up demand for an afternoon service at a lower price than the standard overnight price.

The financial people got their backs up. It doesn't compute, they told the marketing managers. Why should we buy into a service that's going to drop our margins?

The marketing managers said there was no way to forecast a totally new service with any degree of accuracy. Well, said the financial managers, can you tell us how much volume next-afternoon service is going to take from the next-morning or two-day business? No, the marketing managers said, but our *hunch* is that we will gain business rather than cut up our current pie.

The marketing managers had it their way. They plunged ahead with the new next-afternoon service, and it worked. The new service did not reduce existing volume: It enlarged the FedEx market and solidified the company's position as market leader.

As Mike Glenn, senior vice president of marketing, customer service, and corporate communications, said, "I think Fred has ingrained his philosophy in the corporation: If you know something is right, go ahead and make the decision to do it even if the organization may not be totally prepared to adapt at that point in time. Only if you say we are going to do something by X date will people do what they need to do to get it done....And we have taken some risks in that regard with some new services and pricing structures. Financial models have suggested that the new services wouldn't work.

"Well, guess what?" he continued. "Once our people know the price we're charging and what the costs are, and once they commit to making it work, they find some way to do it. If we had looked only at the financial model, we probably wouldn't have moved ahead with next-afternoon service."

It's rare to find companies in which managers have the latitude to make key decisions affecting the company's success. Normally, CEOs and their staffs reserve that sort of decision exclusively for the executive suite, under the assumption that lower-level managers haven't the experience to come up with educated hunches. At FedEx, managers follow their intuitions—it is expected of them.

As Mike Glenn goes on to say, "Because FedEx is a big company, outsiders may think we're not entrepreneurial. They're wrong. There's still a tremendous amount of entrepreneurial spirit inside the company. I told Fred that one of the rewarding elements of my job, and for the people reporting to me, is executive management's willingness to allow us to make key decisions even though the numbers speak against it….You might say, 'You know, I can't quite make the numbers work, but I still believe this is the right thing to do.' And once we show how and why our idea will fly, if it's sound, we get the go-ahead.

"Here's an example," he went on. "We might suggest spending $5 million or more on an advertising campaign. Our chief financial officer could then counter, 'If you didn't need to spend the money, that would be $5 million more for the bottom line.' Well, I can't put an argument on the table that says that $5 million is going to produce $25 million in added sales in this fiscal year. But I know it's the right thing to do. And we do it."

It was Mike Glenn, as a matter of fact, who helped champion changing the company's name from Federal Express to FedEx. He pointed out that customers, on their own, already referred to the company as "FedEx," and that with the company's international push, the word "Federal" might prove a liability. Although many in the company resisted his idea, he did prevail in the end. The marketing department suggested that as part of the name change, the company could save money by painting equipment with white rather than purple paint, which is heavier on account of high lead content. Aside from being lighter in weight, the white also requires less maintenance.

Dave Rebholz, FedEx's senior vice president, sales and trade services, adds, "The higher the risk decision, the more you want to take a hard look at it. Most decisions have some risk, and they're not going to shut the company down if you make a mistake.

"We train our people to be decisive...If you make a mistake we're quick to say it was a mistake; let's shut down and move on—something as simple as a marketing promotion, a pricing decision, a retail network change, anything. Let's act based on what we know at the time and our good judgment about the customer. Doing it this way, we've made mistakes. But we have a hell of a high batting average."

NUMEROCRACY— THE DETERMINATION TO LET HUNCHES OVERRULE THE FINANCIAL EXPERTS

It doesn't take much imagination to predict what would have happened to FedEx in the spring of 1973 had financial specialists been making the FedEx do-or-die decision. They would have shut down the company a few minutes after midnight on March 12. That's assuming they would have allowed the idea to fly from the drawing board, at all.

Quantoids and numerocrats have their place, a vital one, in any business. When they evaluate the potential of an investment, they examine return on investment, cash flow, capital requirements, internal rate of return, present value, and so on. There is nothing wrong with this, so far as it goes. But just how far is that? Like Fred Smith, a CEO (and certainly an entrepreneurial CEO) must never forget that how far the numbers go is his or her decision. You cannot leave decisions to the financial forecasters.

A financial forecast includes two kinds of numbers: revenues and costs. Anticipating costs is reasonably straightforward. Revenue is another matter. Nobody truly knows what revenues will be. Sure, the marketing and sales people can make estimates, but they make estimates based on given market conditions. When conditions change, as they so often do, those estimates are worthless.

Now of course it's always important to know the numbers. All sales and operations managers should know the break-even points of their product and service lines, for example, along with their budgeted expenses. But key decisions about whether or not a product line or service should be added, invested in, or discontinued is not a decision that may be left to the number crunchers. That's what true leaders are for. Those who have the right blend of experience and smarts know instinctively which courses of action are right or wrong for their companies. While they sometimes make the wrong calls, more often than not their judgments are sound.

Take, for instance, the decision Fred Smith and his executive team reached to offer an earlier delivery hour: instead of noon, 10:30 a.m. The financial people had it all figured out. The 10:30 a.m. service would siphon precisely X dollars in sales—the figure doesn't matter—from the standard overnight service; moreover, the new service would never generate enough business to pay for itself.

They were wrong on both counts. Count one: The new service, 10:30 a.m. guaranteed delivery, opened yet another segment of the market that most executives didn't think was there. Smith had seen it, but few agreed with him. Count two: The success of the earlier service helped generate more than adequate income to cover its extra costs. The service became yet another profit center. Later, following much the same sort of debate, the company would introduce 8:00 a.m. delivery, and this, too, would prove successful.

Incidentally, that illustrates the rule-changing concept we looked at in Chapter 6: The critical attribute of successful change is that it benefits the customer. If your business doesn't continually focus on benefits to your customers, another business will. Remember when fast-food restaurants wanted to be so "efficient" that none would let you 'have it your way?' It's not at all difficult to imagine the financial people arguing that it would be way too expensive to make custom hamburgers. By hesitating too long, McDonald's opened the door to a new competitor—Burger King. Remember "Hold the pickles, hold the lettuce, special orders don't upset us."

The financial people—because their focus is so narrowly directed to the bottom line—often miss crucial aspects of a profitable big picture. For example, a few FedEx managers have asked me to appeal to Fred Smith to retreat from his unassailable position of no layoffs. My initial inclination was to do so, because, like the other FedEx managers, I had seen other companies' cost savings justify their layoffs. I reconsidered. I began to realize the value of the no-layoff philosophy, the powerful signal it sends to the 120,000 FedEx employees. FedEx employee loyalty is world-class. I now agree that FedEx should support the policy because its benefits far exceed any imaginable cost savings. It is a decision that forsakes short-term gain for greater—much greater—long-term benefits.

Nevertheless, I fully appreciate that financial professionals would challenge the philosophy; their entire thrust must be to maintain and improve the numbers. That's what they get paid to do. Management must temper that judgment with a broader perspective of what is right for the company.

If you want to follow your instincts and challenge the assumptions of associates and the business community, you will need the faith of Mother Theresa and the raw determination of Bill Gates.

Understand That Every Change Has Its Gestation Period.
Like Fred Smith, whose first tries ended in disappointment, you
may need to go back to the drawing board, reconfigure an approach,
and then plow ahead forcefully. Or, you may simply need to nurture
the idea and wait for the ripeness of time. There will be pressure to
terminate, especially from the financial people. Don't cave in.

**If Possible, Test Your Idea before You Commit to a Course
of Action.** Most companies run samples through production to see
if they can manufacture high-quality products at budgeted costs.
Marketing managers then give those test models to customers to
see how the customers react. You can do the same, even with a service. Only then, after your judgment has been verified, should you
move ahead with full-scale production.

**Above All, Do Not Abandon Your Fight to Turn an Idea into
a Reality Even If You Are Not Totally and Absolutely Convinced
Your Idea Is Sound.** You should be able to stand the suspense:
It's a part of what you're being paid for. Remember, too, that the
more people you can get to find your idea's weak points, the better
set you'll be to make appropriate adjustments. And don't discourage
your financial people from thoroughly investigating the financial via-
bility of the idea. That is their job; if you disparage their efforts, they
will be reluctant to tell you the truth. That will be the kiss of death.
The last thing you want is people afraid to tell you the truth.

**Because Speed Is So Strategically Important, You Must
Develop Rapid Feedback Systems.** I'm not advocating analyzing
to the point of paralyzing your operations, but you do need to know
the impact—good or bad—of your decisions as soon as possible.
Make the most of sales data and toll-free customer hotlines to
extrapolate your future sooner rather than later.

A CHECKLIST FOR MANAGERS

Challenging the authority of numbers is a difficult business, and only those managers utterly determined to succeed should attempt it. Does your company encourage people to listen to and trust their instincts?

1. When the numbers are all wrong, and everyone else tells you to stop, do you have the courage to stick to your guns?

2. Do your executives know that they can count on your support—even when their hunches don't have the financial experts' support? Can you describe situations in which your executives followed their hunches despite discouraging financial forecasts?

3. When you think that you have a really promising hunch, do you envision new sources of revenue and newly configured cost structures?

4. When you follow a hunch—completely unsupported by financial evidence—and it fails, do you approach the problem from another angle, or do you shelve it permanently?

5. Have you encouraged your financial people to take unconventional approaches when they assess inventive proposals? Truly new businesses don't always look promising at first.

6. Are financial analyses—return on investment, break-even analysis, and the like—checkpoints or do they state the final word?

CHAPTER 10

Letting Go Is Hard to Do

---

*H*ave you ever had to take remedial action to rescue your company from a venture that failed to meet your expectations?

*I*n the face of impending disaster, have you had the presence of mind to discontinue a high-investment initiative before it was too late? Describe the strategies you tried before you actually pulled the plug. Did you wait too long?

*H*ow long did you wait to take definitive action once you realized that a money-losing venture could not be turned in a profitable direction?

It happens occasionally, of course, that both your gut instinct and your financial models lead you astray. ZapMail, FedEx's disappointing experiment in state-of-the-art, satellite-connected, faxed-document, to-the-door delivery, failed when low-cost fax machines flooded the business market. Within two years of its launch, FedEx shut ZapMail down, wrote off the losses, and reassigned thousands of ZapMail employees to other tasks.

Why after two years? Why not one, or four? This chapter looks at the agonizing question that all creative, ambitious companies face sooner or later—or should face if they are worthy of being called entrepreneurial. Call it Gresham's Question: So, do we quit trying? When?

At FedEx, people ask that question quite frequently. The culture is truly entrepreneurial; you only have to think of the company's successful breakthroughs: the first hub-and-spoke system, the proprietary fleet of aircraft, the television ads that focus on FedEx technology (itself innovative) rather than on its package delivery, and many more. Nevertheless, FedEx has from the start paid close attention to the consequences of its innovations. Some are what I call "unintended," others "self-inflicted," and still others "self-corrected." Let's take a look at all three.

ANTICIPATING THE UNFORESEEABLE— UNINTENDED CONSEQUENCES

Gresham's Question is actually a bit misleading. The choice between "holding 'em" or "folding 'em" invariably sends us off into realms of contingency where nothing—certainly not "success" or "failure"—is certain or forever, but where, on the contrary, all outcomes are in changing shades of gray. To put it simply, you can't suspend the law of unintended consequences. Still, it's a mistake to assume that all such consequences will be bad.

The story of FedEx's 1984 entry into the global market offers good examples of the mixed bag of unknowables. That same year, FedEx purchased the Minneapolis-based Gelco Express, a package courier business that served more than 80 countries worldwide. Several other acquisitions, in the United Kingdom, Holland, and the United Arab Emirates, quickly followed.

Then, in 1989, Smith made his controversial decision to buy Flying Tigers Airline. FedEx paid a total of $880 million. Some market analysts asserted that FedEx was making some risky moves. Smith disagreed. "It's a big challenge," he said, "no question. I don't know that it's a bet-the-company move. We get a lot of hard assets with the acquisition." Other analysts agreed with Smith, arguing that a company would normally need dozens of years to build the solid international routes that Flying Tigers had at the time of the acquisition.

One consequence of the purchase Smith knew about. To meet the Federal Aviation Administration's maintenance guidelines, many of Flying Tigers' 747 jumbo jets needed overhauls that would cost FedEx another $100 million.

A further consequence, however, was only dimly, if at all, foreseen: the unionization of all FedEx pilots. The merger brought almost 1,000 Flying Tiger pilots into the FedEx family, and every one of them was a union member with legal seniority rights. FedEx already employed 1,000 pilots with seniority rights of their own, which Smith had pledged to protect. It was a recipe for a train wreck. FedEx reluctantly merged all 2,000 pilots into a single seniority list, thereby bumping many FedEx pilots down the seniority roster. They immediately began to lobby for union representation. Then, pilots split their votes, edging out the pilots who wished to remain union free.

But it was in Europe and Asia, in the package-delivery business itself, that the law of unintended consequences came down hard. To many people, it looked just like Murphy's Law: If something can go wrong, it will.

Abroad, FedEx's major competitor was DHL. Although the brown-suited, brown-van company didn't inaugurate air service until 1982, it grew briskly, plowing its vast resources into building a major presence in the overnight air-express business. By the 1990s, UPS had acquired eight small air cargo companies in Europe and Asia. UPS was able to deliver packages in almost 200 countries, and it wasn't FedEx's only rival. DHL, headquartered in Brussels and partially owned by Lufthansa and Japan Air Lines, claimed 40 percent of continental Europe's overnight package-delivery business, with a somewhat greater market share for delivery of all America-bound express air cargo. Its entrenched New York-to-London express route and its 200-plus airplanes serving almost 200 countries worldwide, competed head-to-head with FedEx. It was yet another formidable competitor.

FedEx had many competitors. TNT, an Australian air cargo carrier with annual sales of $4.4 billion, flew in the same markets as FedEx, UPS, and DHL. Major passenger airlines battled for the same air cargo dollars, loading packages in the bellies of their airplanes and charging substantially lower rates. So, from a competitive standpoint, FedEx was active in an arena against powerful and extremely competitive interests.

There was yet another problem: Flying Tigers Airlines used local freight forwarders to deliver packages on the ground, handle customs duties, and provide paperwork on the cargo. When FedEx bought Flying Tigers, the freight forwarders, who had a lot of pull with overseas customers, feared that FedEx would put many of them out of business. To appease that influential group, FedEx promised to limit package weight to 150 pounds. That cut into the company's profits, since the heavier packages yielded higher profit margins. Still not satisfied, the freight forwarders asked FedEx to limit package weights to 30 pounds. When FedEx refused, many freight forwarders shifted business to competitors, adding to FedEx's miseries.

APPLYING TOURNIQUETS— SELF-INFLICTED CONSEQUENCES

FedEx compounded its already severe problems by trying to impose its traditions upon unsuspecting foreign partners and customers. Its tendency to treat everybody the same way danger-ously ignored many sharp cultural variations among countries. Europeans resented the brash Americans with their get-the-job-done-now attitude.

As Joe McCarty, senior vice president of Latin America and the Caribbean, said, "We didn't recognize cultural differences for the longest time....In Germany, for instance, when you said to first-line managers, 'The key part of your job is to ride with the couriers and check their performance,' the German managers would answer, 'You must be joking. I am the manager. I don't do those things.'"

When the company tried to establish a hub in Frankfurt, Germany, the Germans refused to lift nighttime curfews, and FedEx relocated the hub site to Brussels. The company found that tradition was hard to crack in Europe.

That kind of management was typical of hard-charging FedEx managers trained to get the job done at any cost. But in Germany and other countries where the culture distinctly separates social classes, the Memphis way couldn't work, despite all efforts to the contrary.

By the end of 1991, FedEx's operating losses for its first three years in the international market exceeded $600 million. FedEx flights often flew to Tokyo half empty because of the 70-pound limit. The European story was much the same. The company had poured $1.5 billion into its international venture, and it was starting to hemorrhage corporate profits. In 1991 it recorded its first quarterly operating loss since 1978: a staggering $105 million.

Hold 'em, or fold 'em? By the close of 1991 it was apparent that FedEx had to act quickly to stanch the flow of red ink. Smith was prepared to take the drastic steps. He said, "Our domestic businesses in Europe have simply not provided the synergies with our international business. The operations needed to support our intra-European service have been extremely costly, and we have not generated adequate revenues to cover our costs. In addition, the market in Europe has not developed express traffic as quickly as we had expected it to."

In swift moves, FedEx jettisoned its domestic and intra-European operations, closed the Brussels hub, and sought new employment at other companies for more than 6,500 people who had worked in its European operations taking a quarterly charge of $254 million. FedEx pared itself down to a reasonably svelte 2,600 employees working in 16 key European cities. The company didn't simply fold and leave the game.

As Tom Oliver, FedEx's former executive vice president, international operations, put it, "It's important to understand what we are doing and what we are not doing. We still pick up a package in Rome, Georgia, and fly it to Paris, France. We still pick up a package in Paris, France, and fly it to Rome, Georgia. But we will not pick up a package in Paris, France, and fly it to Rome, Italy."

Robert Marcin, a partner in a money management company which manages a few million shares of clients' FedEx equities, expressed good feelings about the downsizing. "It [Europe] is a very small part of the company that is causing a lot of pain and grief. They kept saying they would never let it get out of hand....What they have done is to admit to that, and Fred has shown his ability to be flexible..."

FINDING THE RIGHT REMEDIES— SELF-CORRECTED CONSEQUENCES

FedEx did not let its disappointing European results discourage it. The company had learned painful but beneficial lessons, among them that quitting and hanging in there are not the only alternatives. The company retreated to gather its thoughts, develop a new plan, and make another try. On the culture-clash front, as Joe McCarty said, "It took us a while to find the balance between offending people saying, 'You are trying to Americanize us,' while helping them to understand that FedEx is a global company. We have had many group employee meetings, and we have sponsored a lot of training programs. FedEx has provided endless English language training at our cost and we have given employees who complete the course a pay premium. We have also promoted them into the management ranks. Our management development courses stress the cultures of the countries where our people work."

Cultural differences matter from everyone's point of view: Many foreigners violate American cultural norms that FedEx employees consider sacred. In Japan, for example, precious few women have joined management ranks. In McCarty's own words, "We have been successful in Japan in moving some women into management positions. The women are very reluctant to be seen outside the norm. Men resent working with female peers at the management level. In this culture, you must be willing to compromise. In Japan, women in management roles are generally not accepted."

Another example of a cultural mismatch was the use of FedEx's Survey Feedback Action (SFA) in Japan. That survey, conducted annually in the United States, examines employee attitudes toward a broad range of issues, including their opinions of their bosses.

Here's McCarty again: "We were told in Japan that it was meaningless to survey our Japanese employees because they think as a group. The American tradition of individualism is not welcome in Japan. Japanese employees work together and develop opinions based on the consensus of the group...If the employees like their bosses, they would rate them uniformly high. If they don't like them, they rate them uniformly low. What you don't see is one employee rating his supervisor high, and another rating him low. That doesn't happen. However, once we said, 'Employee ratings are the core of FedEx,' and started using the surveys, we found the Japanese to be just as interested in rating their managers' merit— as individuals, not as a group."

FedEx also learned what isn't always obvious in such nontraditional cultures as America's—that religion permeates life—even at work. In the Middle East, for example, all FedEx locations have prayer rooms in which Muslims may carry out their religious obligations. Its operations are now built around their thrice-daily prayer schedules.

FedEx's strength has been its ability to learn and benefit from the challenging lessons of its early forays into foreign markets. The company redesigned its strategies in ways that complement each culture's preferences, and now it is enjoying successful growth in both Europe and Asia.

Not only does the company do everything within its power to wring every lesson possible from its mistakes, it also evaluates prospective employees in terms of their ability to assess those disappointments. Rather than shrink from acknowledging such failures, for example, some FedEx managers will ask certain applicants to review the ZapMail case and submit their own suggestions for appropriate actions. What, FedEx asks those applicants, would you have done had you been working for FedEx when we were embroiled in ZapMail?

FedEx learned through its ZapMail venture and its initial foray into the international arena that "there's a time to hold 'em and a time to fold 'em"—and a time to do something in between. Some of those lessons were painful. The company lost a great deal of money, and then either made needed adjustments to stay in business—as in its overseas business—or stopped the service entirely—as in its ZapMail venture.

There is a fine line separating success and failure—for ZapMail or any venture. That's true. But it's also true that the line may be constantly moving, that it may be partially porous, or that it may not be there at all. If you throw in the towel too soon, a promising venture may never get off the ground; if you hold on too long, your company can lose a lot of money, possibly even fail. The question becomes: Where do you draw the line?

It's not an easy question to answer: Its resolution is mostly subjective. Like your original instinct, the answer may be equally fuzzy, coming from the gut and heart, but not from the brain. There are certain valuable lessons you can learn from FedEx's experiences:

Your Gut Instincts Could Be Right on Target for Whatever New Service or Product You Itch to Bring to Market. The financial picture may even support your conclusions. Fellow employees may heartily endorse your efforts. Everything seems right, doesn't it?

You can plunge ahead too quickly with a new proposal or wait too long and lose your competitive advantage. FedEx's philosophy has always tended toward the "move-quickly" side. Its managers believe that once your foot is in the door, you can always go back to the new product or service and fine-tune it.

FedEx has never been slow to respond to opportunities. Although it stepped into some pretty hot water in Europe, had it waited to go international, UPS, DHL, and others may have prevented FedEx from gaining any market in Europe.

If Your Organization Doesn't Have an Open Culture— Where Employees Speak Their Minds without Fear of Reprisal—You Will Hear Only What Employees Think You Want to Hear. Say you have just taken over an organization where your predecessor surrounded himself with yes-people. Your first job is to create an environment where you encourage and reward employees who speak their minds. By the way, if you can't recall anyone disagreeing with you lately, you may have a yes-people problem. As you grow more powerful within your organization you also grow more likely to misread situations. Your jokes become funnier, your ideas more profound, and people are less likely to tell you that you don't have any clothes on. Knowing when to hold 'em and when to fold 'em requires a lot of valuable insights from other people.

....

A CHECKLIST FOR MANAGERS

No company can escape forever the specter of a setback or two. The features that separate the winners from the also-rans is the way they prepare for new undertakings and the way they respond to disappointing results. Consider your company in light of your answers to the following questions:

1. Have you ever had to take remedial action to rescue your company from a venture that threatened your future?

2. In the face of impending disaster, have you had the presence of mind to discontinue a high-investment initiative before it was too late? Describe the strategies you tried before you actually pulled the plug. Did you wait too long?

3. If a project you backed—in spite of the caveats put forth by other executives—performed badly, have you resisted acknowledging your mistake?

4. When your executives indicated that a project was a drain on the company's resources, how did you react? How long did it take you to redirect the company?

5. Have you learned how to examine disappointing ventures with a cool and dispassionate eye?

6. How long did you wait to take definitive action once you realized that a money-losing venture could not be turned in a profitable direction?

7. When the company has declared a certain initiative to be a failure, did individuals feel guilty and suffer within the organization because of their association with that failure?

....

CHAPTER 11

The Image Is the Reality (If You Work at It)

Is there a good match between your company's image and its products or services?

Do you take advantage of your company's successes and use them to promote a corporate image of excellence?

Have you made sure that your packaging, advertising, collateral materials—even your invoices—promote the image you want to present?

How does your image compare with your competitors'? Do your customers agree with your assessment?

Gordon Baer, a nationally recognized photojournalist and trainer, tells a story about a seminar he conducted a few years ago. When he came to a blank spot in his carousel of slides, he apologized to his class, saying that his associate had "FedExed" the slide the day before and that it was due to arrive any minute. As if on cue, a FedEx courier walked into the classroom and delivered the missing slide. A round of applause, but no sense of surprise, greeted the navy-and-orange clad figure. Baer inserted the slide into the carousel and continued his lecture.

FedEx is what it does. Lots of people want their packages delivered overnight, to the right address, undamaged, but few say, "let's UPS them" or "Emery them" or "Airborne Express them." What people do say is, "FedEx them." They say it even at the competition's shop. A consultant I know, working with UPS' air operations, reports that high-ranking executives have confided that time and time again UPS customers call and ask UPS to "FedEx" packages for them—a considerable compliment to FedEx. And a teeth-grinding experience for UPS.

At FedEx and in its market, the name is the game. And the converse is also true: The game is the name. This interchangeability of word and deed, of utterance and act, is a priceless asset for a company. And in FedEx's case it's a hard-earned asset. How has FedEx achieved that remarkable position? It strives always to maintain an image that works overtime, that won't fade, that delivers more and more, and that will not compromise.

THE COMPANY AS VERB—
AN IMAGE THAT WORKS OVERTIME

The public, having a short memory, very likely views FedEx as one of those benevolent behemoths that conquered its markets aeons ago and now spends its time swatting off rivals with the ineffable ease of an elephant flapping its ears. Not much of that illusion matches reality. True, FedEx has been "big," in at least one sense, from its earliest days. Fred Smith started the company with $42 million in venture capital, making it the largest venture capital start-up in 1974. In spite of that large cash infusion, however, FedEx's story traces a roller-coaster course that is familiar to many successful start-ups. During the early years, while he struggled to establish a new industry, Smith was engaged in a continuous search for capital: from Wall Street, banks, and private investors. From time to time the company was so starved for cash that, legend has it, Smith once raised the week's payroll at the gambling tables of a Las Vegas casino.

FedEx has always been a street-smart, self-reliant, successful-against-all-odds company. Its rich history supports, if not always visibly, the FedEx image. Its image rings true everywhere: among companies on the Fortune 500, and, more important, among companies not on the Fortune 500. But no company—no matter its size or age—can afford the costs associated with missed production schedules.

Most important of all, perhaps, the image rings true for FedEx employees. FedEx people understand their company's history, and they identify with it. That knowledge instills a sense of pride and belonging: essential attributes of a company that needs continually to attract top job candidates and keep everyone's morale high. People want to work for companies with exemplary reputations in their communities. From the moment they start working with FedEx as sorters or telephone representatives, new employees feel part of a vital organization that plays a significant role not only in the local community but also in the business world as a whole. In a media-dominated culture, FedEx is a celebrity, and a little bit of that celebrity rubs off on everyone who works for it. For contrast, think of the U.S. Postal Service and its odd way of producing "disgruntled" employees.

How did FedEx become a verb?

- It was first in the overnight package-delivery business.

- It was the first package carrier to have a fleet comprising airplanes, crews, and ground support. UPS had a ground fleet before FedEx but had no air fleet until after FedEx had started its operation.

- It was the first carrier to guarantee absolutely, positively overnight delivery or your money back.

- It was the first carrier to introduce time-definite freight delivery.

- It was the first overnight package-delivery business to launch a national television campaign, "America, You've Got a New Airline."

- It was the first service company to win the prestigious Malcolm Baldrige National Quality Award in the service category.

- It was the first carrier to outfit its pickup and delivery vans with sophisticated electronic tracking gear.

- It was the first carrier to allow customers to call for pickups.

- It was the first commercial all-cargo company to employ a staff meteorologist.

- Above all FedEx is almost always on time. Yes, it does miss occasionally, but usually only when such drastic events as hurricanes intervene.

To send a package overnight these days still means to "FedEx it." On June 23, 1994, to further establish the FedEx name as the equivalent of overnight delivery, Federal Express both acknowledged and seized its rightful image in the market by making "FedEx" its official brand name. The company unveiled the new paint scheme for every vehicle and airplane in its global fleet with the new logo, and with its new motto, "The World On Time."

FedEx has combined marketing, customer service, public relations, and employee communications under one umbrella organization managed by Michael Glenn, senior vice president, worldwide marketing, customer service, and corporate communications. Its purpose is to pursue small customers for increased market share. As Glenn says, "It's marketing's job to keep those customers informed and motivated to use FedEx...Customer service has a similar mission...Exceed customer expectations...Employee communications keep our various employee groups informed about what is going on...so they can be better prepared to do their jobs...Public relations has the responsibility of keeping our customers and shareholders informed about the company."

To make your own company's name synonymous with what it does, you should take note. Here's what it takes: time, daring (all those firsts!), hard work, smart work, and lots of luck.

ENERGETICALLY PRESERVING YOUR PUBLIC PERSONA— AN IMAGE THAT WON'T FADE

It happens all too frequently. Dishonest telemarketers inform unsuspecting victims they are winners of, say, a free automobile. All they need to do to collect their prize is send in "registration" fees, by FedEx. The victims, as greedy as their victimizers but not so sly, are only too happy to send off their checks in the purple and orange envelopes. Weeks later they receive a toy car.

Now, thanks to FedEx, potential victims of telemarketing fraud have a way to fight back: In 1987, FedEx initiated a communications effort aimed at stopping deceptive telemarketing practices. The company's Account Confirmation Hotline provides potential victims of fraud with a telephone number to call if they are suspicious of telemarketing come-ons. Trained customer service agents have a variety of remedies ranging from advice on how to handle telemarketing fraud to connecting customers with the country's National Fraud Information Center—at FedEx's expense.

That service has produced dramatic results. In March 1993, for example, the FBI shut down hundreds of boiler room telemarketing operations, crediting FedEx's Account Confirmation Hotline with supplying much of the needed information.

A (proprietary) word that's also a significant and widely valued deed is an immense commercial asset. But it's also, as history tells us, a wasting asset—or one in constant danger of wasting. Just ask the makers of Kleenex tissues, of Xerox copying machines, of Frigidaire "iceboxes." FedEx knows that keeping its word-deed-image meaningful and bright is a most important task. *Everyone's* task. The PR and advertising people can only confirm what consumers already know. Otherwise the work of image sustenance is a matter of unremitting service: consistent, reliable, inventive, new, price-competitive, and more.

Michael Glenn puts it succinctly: "I often remind people that there are two things required to be a market leader. You must have dominant share of mind, and dominant share of market. Lose either one, and you will eventually lose market leadership." If the service is absolutely dependable overnight pickup and delivery, you say "FedEx." But what's the key word in that description? Dependable. Thus with that one word-association, FedEx and its name have changed their environment from morally neutral to morally charged. Even the Rolling Stones appreciate this. Moving the band's Voodoo Lounge tour from country to country was among the most exacting and complex logistical projects FedEx has ever undertaken. To support this 120-concert world tour through Asia, North and South America, Australia, and Africa, FedEx needed to move 300 tons of fragile equipment that included the world's largest video screen, thousands of lights, instruments, and stage props. Everything had to arrive well before the scheduled concert dates. FedEx devoted three 747s to the task.

But FedEx does more than dependably deliver packages. Its range of services is continually expanding. As we shall see, it has developed real-time tracking systems that instantly show the location of any package—from pickup through delivery. It employs designers to customize packaging systems that can handle anything from tiny, delicate eggs to four-ton water drilling equipment. Not long ago, FedEx designers packaged a giant snowball in a refrigerated container in Appleton, Wisconsin, and managed to get it to Memphis—intact—for a child in St. Jude's Hospital. They have packaged and shipped a windmill from Denmark. They have packaged a five-ton communications satellite and shipped it from Los Angeles to China. And they have designed special cages to ship tigers, rhinoceroses, pandas, and thoroughbred racehorses. That talent and capability is ready and able to help any customer ship anything anywhere.

Thousands of employees stand behind FedEx deliveries: the customer service representatives who take the orders, trace packages, and correct problems; the inventory control specialists who make sure that FedEx has all materials, parts, and supplies it needs to keep running smoothly; and the traffic specialists in the hubs and other company stations who route traffic and make thousands of corrections daily to compensate for bad weather, truck breakdowns, and airplane maintenance—all to ensure the packages are delivered "absolutely, positively overnight."

Again, the question arises: How did the company make this traverse into the realm of moral images?

At the time FedEx was born, the air shipping business was small, about $100 million. Sixty percent of the traffic traveled in and out of such major airports as Atlanta's Hartsfield, Boston's Logan, or Los Angeles International, but 80 percent of the demand lay far outside those areas. People who needed a package quickly had no alternative but to arrange for delivery to the closest metropolitan airport, and then the package might languish at the airport for three or four days before the carrier's customer service agent notified the customer. Once notified, customers would either send a messenger service to collect and bring it to them or they would pick it up themselves. The cost was high in both money and time. Damaged packages and deliveries to wrong addresses were common, and belated deliveries (that is, broken promises) were endemic. But those who relied on the U.S. Postal Service could easily expect to wait four weeks for deliveries.

Smith understood that most businesses—particularly small to midsize companies and start-ups—couldn't afford to carry large parts inventories. They had to rely on outside carriers to keep the parts moving to their docks. How much of an inventory, for example, should high-tech companies carry, when not having such high-value parts as computer microprocessors could mean putting production lines on hold and product life cycles could top out at six months. Smith judged that those businesses would pay a fair price for a self-described reliable, promise-keeping overnight delivery carrier. And he was right.

But then the predictable happened. Customers came to expect that unfailing degree of dependability. It happens everywhere: What customers delight in today they come to view as the norm tomorrow. Travelers considered free breakfasts, newspapers, and coffee delivered to their hotel rooms as treats when those services first appeared. Later, of course, they came to look upon them as standards, and they booked rooms only at hotels that provided the free goodies.

The moral of those moral stories? In the service business, not only do you have to keep your promises—and go on and on keeping them—you have to recognize that the better you are at promising and keeping promises, the more banal each service becomes. You must continue to make more and more promises. And you must keep those promises, watch them become the norm, and then make more promises...It's never easy to keep a moral image gleaming.

KEEPING TRACK OF THE NUMBERS—
AN IMAGE THAT DELIVERS MORE AND MORE

When FedEx became the first service company to win the celebrated Malcolm Baldrige National Quality Award in the service category, Fred Smith played it down. In the eyes of the public the award goes only to the very best American companies, but Smith commented that winning it didn't mean the company was perfect: It indicated only that it had been awarded a license to practice.

It was, of course, worth somewhat more than that, but Smith knows that the public is unforgiving and fickle: No number of Baldrige Awards can change that. That's one reason the company pays such close attention to its Service Quality Indicators (SQIs) and the other measures it has designed to keep its finger on the customers' pulse. As Smith says, "Our service standard is 100 percent...98 percent or 99 percent may be fine for other human endeavors. Our chosen profession is not among them. Our customers expect faultless service...all the time."

Accordingly, every quarter the company interviews 2,400 customers by telephone, and, at its more than 1,000 manned customer service centers, it constantly elicits customer responses through comment cards placed in convenient locations.

FedEx's Service Quality Indicator (SQI) is widely recognized throughout the business community as one of the best-designed barometers of customer satisfaction. It's a weighted index that tracks several factors: right day late, wrong day late, late pickup stops, traces (for packages late or missing in the system), complaints reopened, damaged packages, lost packages, inventory adjustment requested (package contains fewer items than specified), and missing proof of delivery. Since its inception in 1987, the system has produced dramatic improvements in customer service. From that year on, the SQI has remained constant although FedEx has increased its daily package shipment volume from 800,000 to 2.5 million.

Because people at FedEx make decisions that are based on an if-you-can't-measure-it-you-can't-manage-it philosophy, they have developed a comprehensive range of performance measurements that follow every internal operation that could contribute either directly or indirectly to customer problems. The internally focused indices extend beyond the SQI to keep tabs on key aspects of the pickup-sort-delivery process that contribute to the high customer service image the company is so intent upon maintaining. Because of those capabilities to track operations, FedEx was the first global express transportation company to win worldwide certification from the International Standards Organization certification, which, aside from the Baldrige Award, is the most comprehensive quality standard achievable. ISO 9001 certification is another tool the company applies to provide 100-percent customer satisfaction. It means that:

- FedEx has internal processes—to track all packages—from pickup through sort and delivery that ensure the dependability of on-time delivery.

- FedEx has uniform quality standards throughout the process to maintain a consistent service level.

- FedEx can ship any package anywhere in the 90 countries regulated by ISO.

When service is the image, and vice versa, the company must constantly reinforce that message throughout the organization. Customer service centers must be spotlessly clean and well organized;

exceeds most customers' expectations. If managers fail to resolve the problem during that initial call or in the course of that same day, customer satisfaction drops precipitously. Claims analysis identifies the most frequently occurring customer problems and suggests which of those problems FedEx managers should resolve first, second, and so forth. But timely problem correction requires a certain freedom and power in the correctors. FedEx customer service agents (CSA) have authority to remedy complaints up to a certain dollar amount, and they use information databases that enable them to deal with the larger and more complex problems. About 80 to 85 percent of all claims fall within the range the CSAs can remedy on the spot. Most companies believe if you make it difficult for a customer to get satisfaction, the customer will hesitate to complain or will give up without making much noise. FedEx couriers, however, understand that when people have just experienced a loss, they are quite upset: If you want them to remain customers, make sure you don't stonewall them.

A company cannot design and project its image—an admirable image that the public internalizes—with a snap of the fingers. It takes years to accomplish; it takes thoughtful planning; it takes diversion of resources from other company projects; and it takes commitment to fortify the image with an organization that delivers what it promises. Nothing tarnishes an image so quickly and thoroughly as failure to perform.

Here is a synopsis of the major aspects of FedEx's strong, positive image, and how it came to dominate its industry:

- Among its most remarkable accomplishments has been FedEx's becoming a verb. "FedEx it" has become an indelible phrase in the public's lexicon. But the company accomplished more than that: Xerox, after all, is a verb, too. FedEx, however, has managed to get the public to associate the verb with a moral act, the keeping of a promise. Accomplish that, and you've got a world-beater of a company.

■ FedEx has done an exceptional job not only of keeping promises, but also of keeping its brand name in the public eye. Its new identity, FedEx, its new motto, "The World On Time," and its eye-catching company colors splashed across planes, vans, packages, and uniforms, continually remind the buying public about the company—and how good it is.

■ When you think of FedEx you think of innovation: keeping at least one step ahead of the customers' rising expectations. FedEx is always on the lookout for unique or different ways to meet or anticipate customers' requirements. From custom-designed packages to special handling, customers' needs are paramount.

■ FedEx motivates its employees to project the company's image of helpfulness and consideration for both external and internal customers, their fellow employees at the next workstation. That takes persistent, day-in and day-out coaching, training, reinforcement, and promotion from within.

■ Employee empowerment is one of the basic ingredients of customer satisfaction and, consequently, of sustaining a valuable image. A company can satisfy customers only when it first satisfies its employees.

Here is a methodology you can use to help you establish your own company's image:

■ First, find out how the market perceives your company. Does it match your own view? The narrower the gap between those two images the more effective your company is. Survey your customers, potential customers, distributors, competitors, and employees. Most probably, you'll find that your company is known for several things. Quantify the responses, and determine the percentage of responses each factor earned. You may be surprised. You may have thought that customers admired your company for its ability to bring new products to the market. Perhaps the survey will show that customers are much more aware of your company's record for customer service. Surprises are common when a company fails to keep abreast of employees' and customers' perception of it.

■ Next, try to gather the same information relative to your competition. You won't be in a position to survey competitors' employees, but there are market research firms that can gather such data. Nevertheless, you certainly can survey the competition's customers. Compare your results with the competitors'. Those answers will help direct your image-building process. If, for example, the public perceives your chief competitor as much better at bringing new products to market, you may decide to channel your resources and energy toward becoming the manufacturer known for the lowest prices.

■ Ask your customers how you may better serve them. In the survey try to distinguish between how customers view you now —the first step of the survey described in the preceding paragraphs—and how they believe you serve them now.

■ When you define your company's image, remember to make it certain and unambiguous. Nobody—not employees, not customers, and not the general public—can confuse the message, "Absolutely, positively overnight." It is crystal clear.

- Finally, deliver. Do exactly what you said you were going to do—never less. You build your image with words, but you must fortify it with deeds. When I seal a navy and orange FedEx package, I know the recipient will get it "absolutely, positively" tomorrow. I don't worry: That's message clarity.

Beyond that: Do it first. Do it right. Do it with distinction and style.

....

A CHECKLIST FOR MANAGERS

Over the years, FedEx has learned how to maintain an image synonymous with the company itself. "The World On Time" is not an empty promise. It, like the phrase "absolutely, positively overnight," means exactly what it says. To see how your company's image stacks up, consider these questions:

1. Does your company's image match up well with its products or services?

2. Do you take advantage of your company's successes and use them to promote a corporate image of excellence?

3. Do your employees project your company's image?

4. Do your company's products and services deliver unremitting dependability?

5. Have you made sure that your packaging, advertising, collateral materials—even your invoices—promote the image you want to present?

6. Is the image you have established for your company one that can last into the next decade, at least?

7. How does your image compare with your competitors'? Do your customers agree with your assessment? How do you know what your customers think of your company?

....